I0216632

"I am delighted to see this new edition of *The Teachings of Shri Vallabhacharya* by Shyamdas, one of the most knowledgeable and passionate interpreters of Pushti Margiya literature for English readers. Shyamdas's generosity for sharing his vast understanding of the fascinating school of Krishna bhakti known as the Pushti Marg—in person as well as in his writings—was huge. This accurate and readable translation of some of the major works by Shri Vallabhacharya, the sixteenth-century religious philosopher, is a great service to both scholars and seekers alike."

—DAVID L. HABERMAN
Professor of Religious Studies, Indiana University

"This new edition of the *Ṣoḍaśagranthāḥ* or *Sixteen Treatises* of Shri Vallabhacharya, with lucid English translation by the late Pushti Marg aspirant Shyamdas (1953-2013) and a new introduction by the grandson of his revered guru, the late Shri Prathameshji, will be of great value to the Anglophone Pushti Marg aspirant. This volume should serve as a guide to the teachings of Shri Vallabhacharya, understanding that these works were written in a context of active teaching and Sanskrit commentary. This means they should serve as a springboard for further discussion within groups of devotees and as an opportunity to memorize the texts themselves, in order to help pave the path for one's own devotion."

— FREDERICK M. SMITH
Professor of Sanskrit, University of Iowa

"My dear friend Shri Shyamdasji was not only a great scholar of Shri Vallabhacharya's pure non-dual Vedanta, but he was himself a sincere and devoted practitioner of the path of grace. While much has been said about his life, personality, and influence in the bhakti community, there is one contribution that has been overlooked and underappreciated—it was Shyamdasji who, for the first time in the 500+ year history of the Vallabha tradition, has made this profound philosophy of *Shuddhadvaita* (pure non-dualism) available to the wider English speaking world. Were it not for Shyamdasji's tireless efforts in translating the works of Vallabhacharya and other authors of the tradition, these sublime teachings would have remained in the domain of Sanskrit scholars and Indian language readers only. It was Shyamdasji who single-handedly made these rare bhakti teachings available to the whole world. It is this unique contribution that we should all be extremely grateful for."

— MUSTA RAM / IRA SCHEPETIN
Vedantin, Sanskrit Scholar, Author

The Teachings of Shri Vallabhacharya

Also by Shyamdas

Inner Goddess
Loving Wisdom
The Path of Grace
252 Vaishnavas, Parts 1–3
Venu Gita: The Song of the Flute
Ecstatic Couplets: The Yugal Gita
The Amazing Story of Shri Nathji
Krishna's Inner Circle: The Ashta Chaap Poets
The Poems of Rasakhan: Treasure House of Love
In Praise of Vallabh: The Vallabhakhyan of Gopaldas
Ocean of Jewels: The Prameyaratnarnava of Lallu Bhatta
Ocean of Grace: The Teachings of H.H. Goswami Prathameshji
Shri Harirayaji's Shiksha Patra: Forty-one Letters of Spiritual Counsel

The Teachings of Shri Vallabhacharya

Translated by
Shyamdas

Edited by
Vallabhdas

Published by
Pratham Peeth Publications
Saugerties, NY • Kota, Rajasthan
2021

This book is published in the United States by
Pratham Peeth Publications, LLC
under the auspices of
Bade Mathuradheeshji Temple Board
Kota, Rajasthan

The Teachings of Shri Vallabhacharya
3rd edition, 2021
Translated by Shyamdas
Edited by Vallabhdas

ISBN: 978-0-9746768-1-4
Library of Congress Control Number: 2021935685

© Susan Ryan, Mae Ryan, and Hannah Seligson
All rights reserved. No part of this book may be reproduced, copied, stored, or transmitted, in any country, by any means electronic, physical, photocopying, recording or otherwise, without prior written permission of the copyright owners Susan Ryan, Mae Ryan, and Hannah Seligson. Breach of this condition is illegal and punishable by international law. If written permission is granted, portions of this work may be reproduced or quoted, with proper acknowledgment of the translator (Shyamdas), copyright holders (Susan Ryan, Mae Ryan, and Hannah Seligson) and publisher (Pratham Peeth Publications).

For inquiries and information, please contact the publisher:
Pratham Peeth Publications, LLC
email: prathampeethpublications@gmail.com
phone: 813.360.1008

Cover design by Jhumkabai
Cover painting courtesy of The Amit Ambalal Collection

Pratham Grhanidhi
Shri Mathuradheesh Prabhu

Goswami 108 Shri Ranchodarcharya
(Shri Vallabhalalji) "Prathameshji" Maharaj

14th Tilkayat of the Pushtimarg Pratham Peeth
17th generation descendant of Shri Vallabhacharya

Goswami 108 Shri Vitthalnathji
(Shri Lalmaniji) Maharaj

15th Tilkayat of the Pushtimarg Pratham Peeth
18th generation descendant of Shri Vallabhacharya

Goswami Shri Prabhuji (Shri Milan Kumarji) Mahodaya

Pushtimarg Pratham Peeth Yuvaraj
19th generation descendant of Shri Vallabhacharya

Goswami Lalan Ranchodlalji
(Shri Krishnasya Bava)
Pushtimarg Pratham Peeth Yuvaraj-atmaja
20th generation descendant of Shri Vallabhacharya

Contents

Foreward xv
Editor's Note xxxi
Introduction xxxiii

Introductory Meditations:

Maṅgalācaraṇam
Auspicious Beginning 1
Śrī Kṛṣṇa Svarūpa Dhyānam
Shri Krishna's Form 7
Śrīmad Ācāryacaraṇa Svarūpa Dhyānam
Shri Vallabhacharya's Form 9
Śrīviṭṭhalanātha Prabhucaraṇa Dhyānam
Shri Vitthalnathji's Form 11
Śrī Sarvottama Stotram
The Best Recitation 13

Shri Vallabhacharya's *Sixteen Works*:

Śrī Yamunāṣṭakam
In Praise of Shri Yamuna 31
Bāla Bodhaḥ
Instructions for Spiritual Children 39
Siddhānta Muktāvalī
The Pearl Necklace Teachings 51
Puṣṭi Pravāha Maryādā
The Paths of Grace, Mundane Flow,
and Lawful Limitations 65
Siddhānta Rahasyam
The Secret Doctrine 79

Navaratnam
Nine Jewels 85
Antaḥkaraṇa Prabodhaḥ
An Appeal to My Heart 91
Viveka Dhairyāśrayaḥ
Wisdom, Perseverance, and Refuge 99
Kṛṣṇāśraya Stotram
Refuge in Krishna 109
Catuḥ Ślokī
Four Verses 117
Bhakti Vardhinī
How to Increase Devotion 121
Jala Bhedaḥ
Differences in Waters 129
Pañca Padyāni
Five Lines 141
Saṃnyāsa Nirṇayaḥ
My Conclusions on Renunciation 147
Nirodha Lakṣaṇam
Nirodha, Bound by Hari 161
Sevā Phalam Sa-Vivaraṇam
The Rewards of Seva 173

Concluding Works:

Śrī Madhurāṣṭakam
The Song of Sweetness 183
Śikṣā Padyāni
The Last Teachings 189
Viveka Dhairyāśrayaḥ commentary
Lover's Life 193
About the Translator 227

प्रथमेश

Vijayate Śrīman Mathurādhīśa Prabhuḥ

॥ विजयते श्रीमन्मथुराधीशप्रभुः ॥

GOSWAMI SHRI MILAN KUMAR
Shuddhadvaita Pratham Peeth
Kota • Jatipura • Mumbai • Kolkata
milangoswami@gmail.com

Foreward

श्रीमद्-वल्लभनामधेय सदृशो भावि न भूतोऽस्त्यपि ।

śrīmad-vallabha-nāmadheya sadṛśo bhāvi na bhūto'styapi

There never has been and never will be another guru and acharya like Shri Vallabh. Who other than Shrimad Vallabh could impart knowledge of *Pushti Purushottama*—the grace filled supreme being? Who besides Shri Vallabh could impart knowledge of Bhagavan Shri Krishna's greatness, and entrust Bhagavan's true form (*svarūpa*) to divine souls, so that they can lovingly serve him with *sevā*—devoted service? Shri Vallabh alone is such a treasure of grace.

Shri Gusainji has praised his father, Shri Vallabh, as "*śrīkṛṣṇa-jñānado guruḥ*—the guru who gives understanding of Shri Krishna"[1] and noted, "*adeya-dāna-dakṣaśca mahodāra caritravāṇ*—He is brilliant at giving the ungivable, and his character is full of generosity."[2]

Shri Acharya-charana,[3] Shri Vallabh, manifested these *16 Works* to demonstrate his grace upon divine souls of this age, so that they would be able to do Shri Krishna's seva, filled not only with knowledge of Shri Krishna's greatness, but also the bliss that arises after such wisdom dawns.

śrīmad-ācārya-caraṇāḥ svīyānāṁ bhakti-siddhaye
akārṣuḥ ṣoḍaśa-granthān sva-siddhāntārtha-bodhakān.

Shri Dvarkesh-charana, in the above passage from his *Anvayabodhinī* commentary on the *Yamunāṣṭakam*, writes that Shri Vallabhacharya-charana composed the *16 Works* "to perfect his bhaktas' devotion and impart knowledge of his philosophy to them."

Just as there are sixteen Vedic rites of passage, called *samskaras*, these *16 Works* are samskaras for Pushtimargiya followers. Vaishnavas become cultured through studying these texts and can then spend their grace filled lives immersed in divine service.

There are sixteen types of ornamentation, or shringar (*śṛngāra*), renowned in the Indian tradition. The instructions of Shri Acharya-charana found in these *16 Works* are a kind of divine ornamentation that adorn the hearts of Vaishnavas. The teachings are beautifully arranged so as to perfect and refine us.

For Vaishnavas, Shri Acharya-charana's *16 Works* grant access to a devotional lifestyle in which the darkness of ignorance is removed by the light of knowledge. Just as the moon has sixteen skillful arts (*kalā*) which spread light and eradicate darkness, these *16 Works* are the moon that lights the grace filled devotional path for all who would follow it.

Just as Shri Krishna manifested the *Shrimad Bhagavad Gita* to remove Arjuna's delusions, these *16 Works* are equal to the *Gita*, in that they dispel all ignorance for grace filled souls. We can also call the *16 Works*, "*The Shrimad Vallabha Gita.*" Like the *Gita*, this text resides in the home of every Vaishnava in the Pushti Sampradaya.

We can also view the *16 Works* from another angle, as being equal to the *Shrimad Bhagavat* scripture. It is believed that the *Shrimad Bhagavat* is the physical embodiment of Shri Krishna: "*teneyaṁ vāṅgamayī mūrtiḥ pratyakṣā vartate hare*" (*Bhagavat Māhātmya* 3.63). In the same way, these *16 Works* are the very form of Shri Vallabha in words. As Shri Dvarkeshji described in *Anvayabodhinī*, his commentary on *Yamunāṣṭakam*, "*avatāra daśāyāṁ tu udhdṛtī rūpa-darśanāt iha nāmātmakair-granthaiḥ sva-dāsānāṁ sadodhdṛtiḥ*—At the time of Shrimad Acharya-charana's incarnation, one could be uplifted just by seeing his form. Now his close devotees are uplifted through the words of these texts."

One *kīrtan* (song) by Shri Harirayaji, "*kara mana śrī vallabha aṅgana dhyāna*—O my heart! Meditate upon the form of Shri Vallabh," further illuminates this subject. Shri Harirayaji explains in this kirtan that the *16 Works* are the form of Shri Vallabh. He describes how each of the *16 Works* corresponds to a particular limb of Shri Vallabh's body.

Shri Acharyacharana wrote in his text *Bhāgavatārtha Prakaraṇa*, "*puruṣe dvādaśatvaṁ hi sakthau bāhū śiro'ntaram.*"

This and many other passages indicate that the twelve cantos of the *Shrimad Bhagavat* are the twelve limbs of Prabhu. Accordingly, here too the *16 Works* of Shri Vallabh are the very limbs of his body. These passages prove that wherever the *16 Works* are present, there too Shrimad Vallabha resides in actual physical form—there is no doubt about it.

Shri Mahaprabhuji composed these works (*granthas*) at different times for various followers, although for some of the *16 Works* we do not have evidence of the exact time or for whom they were composed. The order in which the *16 Works* are listed today is not necessarily the order in which Shri Mahaprabhuji explained them, as evidenced by the year of each composition.

For example, the first grantha, *Śrī Yamunāṣṭakam* (*In Praise of Shri Yamuna*) was composed on Shravan Shukla 3 in Vikram Samvat 1549 (1492 CE), in Shrimad Gokul. It was only a short time thereafter, on Shravan Shukla 11 of the same year, that Shrimad Acharya-charana introduced *Siddhānta Rahasyam*, which is nonetheless arranged as the 5th grantha in the series. *Antaḥkaraṇa Prabodhaḥ* (*An Appeal to My Heart*) was one of the last granthas, created in V.S. 1587 (1530 CE), but it is arranged as the 7th grantha in the series.

Three of our tradition's acharyas—Shri Harirayaji, Shri Purushottamji and Shri Dvarkeshji—have weighed in on the subject of the order of the *16 Works* collection. The standard order accepted today (and followed in this edition) is according to Shri Harirayaji.

Shri Purushottamji's opinion on the order, accepted by Shri Dvarkeshji as well, is slightly different. According to these latter two acharyas, the order is as follows:

1) *Śrī Yamunāṣṭakam*
2) *Bāla Bodhaḥ*
3) *Siddhānta Muktāvalī*
4) *Siddhānta Rahasyam*
5) *Navaratnam*
6) *Antaḥkaraṇa Prabodhaḥ*
7) *Viveka Dhairyāśrayaḥ*
8) *Kṛṣṇāśraya Stotram*
9) *Catuḥ Ślokī*
10) *Puṣṭi Pravāha Maryādā*
11) *Bhakti Vardhinī*
12) *Jala Bhedaḥ*
13) *Pañca Padyāni*
14) *Saṃnyāsa Nirṇayaḥ*
15) *Nirodha Lakṣaṇam*
16) *Sevā Phalam*

Shrimad Acharya's opinion, as attested in his *Tattvārtha Dīpa Nibandha,* is that, "having understood the sacred scriptures, one should serve Shri Krishna with mind, speech and body."[4] The *16 Works* constitute one such sacred scripture that should be known, read, and understood before doing Bhagavat seva. Indeed, Bhagavat seva can be understood as the essence of the entire *16 Works.* Their purpose is essentially to establish teachings relevant to serving the Lord. It is with this devotional mood, or *bhāva,* that Shri Dvarkeshji begins his *Anvayabodhinī* commentary by saying, "And now, the *16 Works* on service to the supreme being."[5]

Shri Vallabh's *16 Works,* a true sacred form embodied in words (*nāmātmaka svarūpa*), reside in the homes of all Vaishnavas. In these modern times, it is extremely important that these teachings, along with their meanings and bhavas, also take root in all Vaishnavas' hearts.

One way or another, a Pushtimargiya Vaishnava is inevitably introduced to the *16 Works* at some point in the course of their life. Typically, children learn to recite *Śrī Yamunāṣṭakam* from hearing it over and over again.

The entire collection of the *16 Works* contains the depths of the living Vaishnava tradition, but because of the lack of time characteristic of our modern lifestyle, not everyone recites the entire *16 Works* from *Yamunāṣṭakam* all the way through *Sevā Phalam*. Most Vaishnavas confine themselves to reciting only *Yamunāṣṭakam*, *Kṛṣṇāśraya*, *Navaratnam*, *Catuh Ślokī*, and *Siddhānta Rahasyam*. Very few are able to recite by heart the other texts like *Bāla Bodhaḥ*, *Puṣṭi Pravāha Maryādā*, *Pañca Padyāni*, and *Saṃnyāsa Nirṇayaḥ*.

If Vaishnavas are unable to even recite all *16 Works*, then fully grasping the texts and their commentaries remains a distant reality. The teachers (*ācāryas*) who have come before us took great pains to write beautiful commentaries. Only some people attempt to read and understand the *16 Works* and their commentaries.

I personally feel that since the *16 Works* are the "true form in name" (*nāmātmaka svarūpa*) of Shri Vallabh, we should place that svarupa fully in our heart through recitation and study. If possible we should recite the *16 Works* from start to finish, but if there is not time to do so every day, one can at least recite one text daily, proceeding one by one to include all *16 Works*. We should read *Bāla Bodhaḥ*, *Jala Bhedaḥ*, and the other works with the same focus we apply when reciting *Yamunāṣṭakam* and the other, more commonly recited texts.

By reciting in this way, bringing Shrimad Vallabh's namatmak svarup into our hearts in the form of the *16 Works*, with meaning and bhava, and serving Bhagavan, our life becomes spritually accomplished.

Now let us take a sacred glimpse together into to the *Shri Vallabha Gita*, this namatmak svarup of Shri Vallabh, with a brief introduction to each of the *16 Works*:

Śrī Yamunāṣṭakam

This lyrical stotra serves as an auspicious introduction (*maṅgalācaraṇa*) to the *16 Works*. Just as an inner current of *dāsya-bhāva*, devotion in the mood of service, flows within the holy Ganga River, so grace filled devotion flows within Shri Yamunaji.

In this text Shri Vallabhacharyaji extols the physical (*ādhibhautika*), the spiritual (*ādhyātmika*), and the divine (*ādhidaivika*) forms of Shri Yamunaji. In each of eight verses, he praises Shri Yamunaji's eight extraordinary specialties, her eight forms of magnificence (*aiśvarya*).

Bāla Bodhaḥ

This work is a synopsis of all philosophies, rather than an exposition of Shri Vallabhacarya's own philosophy. In this work Shri Acharya-charana reflects on the four pursuits of human life: dharma, wealth (*artha*), desire (*kāma*), and liberation (*mokṣa*). Each is explained in simple terms in this text.

The main discussion in this work concerns liberation, which has been depicted both in divine terms by the Vedic texts and in worldly terms by the sages. Worldly liberation is further divided into two variations: independent (through personal effort, according to either Sankhya or Yoga) and dependent (through relying on Vishnu or Shiva as one's benefactor).

Siddhānta Muktāvalī

In this text Shri Acharya-charana outlines the nature of *sevā* (divine service) as well as the means, the secondary rewards, and the main rewards of seva. The kinds of people who do seva are depicted here in terms of the highest, middling, low, and lowest levels of eligibility. The physical (*ādhibhautika*), spiritual (*ādhyātmika*), and divine (*ādhidaivika*) forms of Brahman (ultimate reality) are also described.

Puṣṭi Pravāha Maryādā

In this teaching Shri Vallabh has brilliantly expounded on the differences and subdivisions of souls on the paths of grace (*puṣṭi*), worldly flow (*pravāha*), and lawful limitations (*maryādā*). Grace filled souls can be pure or mixed, and lawful souls can also be mixed. Worldly souls are also of various kinds, including wanderers (*carṣaṇī*), the ignorant (*ajña*), and lastly, the truly wicked (*durjña*).

Siddhānta Rahasyam

This work was spoken to Shri Vallabh by Shri Krishna himself, who manifested before him and instructed him that by taking Brahma Sambandha initiation, the five impurities and obstructions to seva will be eliminated. The main subject of this work is an explanation of the duties of those souls who take Brahma Sambandha.

Navaratnam

In this work Shri Vallabh instructs dedicated souls to relinquish anxiety. Three kinds of dedication are spoken of. The main elucidation of this work is the practices and duties of dedicated souls.

Antaḥkaraṇa Prabodhaḥ

Here Shri Acharya-charana enlightens his dear ones, on the pretext of awakening his inner self. In this instruction, he gives the example of commands he himself received from Bhagavan and explains why one should not lament having forsaken the Lord's commands.

Viveka Dhairyāśrayaḥ

Wisdom, perseverance, and divine refuge are explained in this work. There are nine types of wisdom (*viveka*), including: seeing that every seemingly unfortunate incident is rooted in the wish of Prabhu; accepting that everything that happens is Prabhu's lila; maintaining awareness of mind and speech through reciting the eight-syllable refuge mantra *Shri Krishnah sharanam mama*; not praying for things, etc. Perserverence is to withstand the three types of miseries (worldly, spiritual, and divine). Refuge is to always maintain the bhava that Shri Hari is the refuge, whether in suffering, loss, lack of power, in power, etc.

Kṛṣṇāśraya Stotram

Bhagavan Shri Krishna alone is supreme Brahman and the supreme soul, and so we take only his refuge (*āśraya*). To attain that refuge there are 6 limbs of dharma which should be conducive: time (*kāla*), place (*deśa*), resources (*dravya*), agent (*kartā*), mantra, and action (*karma*). The reward of Krishna-refuge is said to be supreme, from the perspective of the paths of karma, knowledge, bhakti, and even surrender (*prapatti*) as well.

Catuḥ Ślokī

In this work the four pursuits of life for Pushtimargiya Vaishnavas are explained. Dharma is dāsya dharma, the way of servitude, namely Shri Hari's seva. Artha (wealth) is Shri Krishna himself. Kāma is to feel desire, with all the senses, for the auspicious sight (*darśana*) of the Lord and other related experiences. Mokṣa is to become liberated from everything else and become Shri Krishna's, through *sarvātmabhāva*—the state in which one feels Krishna in all things and all things in Krishna.

Bhakti Vardhinī

This work explains the methods by which to strengthen the seed of *bhakti* (devotion), through *kathā* (hearing and reciting sacred names, stories, and teachings) or through a combination of *sevā* (service) and kathā. Renouncing all else, one should reflect on the songs (*kīrtan*) etc. of the path of grace, protect one's personal dharma at home, renounce anything antithetical to Shri Krishna's seva, and perform any activities necessary for livelihood, while fixing one's mind on Shri Hari. After the seed is firm, the individual may experience in progression the states of love (*prema*), attraction (*āsakti*), and addiction (*vyasana*).

Prema is when the allure of anything unrelated is destroyed, and one naturally engages in seva. Āsakti is a lack of taste for the worldly home and the experience of bliss when with Krishna. Vyasana is when one feels a lack of intimacy with worldly non-Vaishnavas and can no longer stand to be without Krishna.

Bhakti Vardhinī advises renouncing the home only after the state of vyasana is attained, at which point the worldly home would otherwise eliminate the precious devotional state of separation (*viprayoga*). This text also describes how the attainment of Prabhu is developed through firm love and supreme devotion for him above all else. It explains that renunciation can lead to impure association and food. Alternatively it is recommended to reside in a place of pilgrimage, to take the association of accomplished bhaktas, and to do seva and sacred reflection (*smaraṇa*), striking a balance between living somewhat close but somewhat removed from others. This is the essence of *Bhakti Vardhinī.*

Jala Bhedaḥ

Drawing from the ancient Vedic text *Kṛṣṇa-yajuḥ Taittirīya-śākhā-saṁhitā* (7.4.12), in this work Shri Acharya-charana compares the bhava of twenty kinds of speakers to twenty types of water. It is not known exactly when, where, or for whom he composed this work. It delineates the best, middling, and lowest natures of various speakers of sacred stories (*Bhagavat-kathā*). Speakers attracted to worldliness are featured in verses 1–5 and speakers desirous of liberation in verses 6–18. The liberated sages described in the scriptures are compared to six types of oceans. What we should learn from this text is what type of speaker we should listen to. The bhava of the speaker comes into the listener, so it is extremely important to choose carefully when selecting a speaker to listen to.

Pañca Padyāni

Similar to the previous work, *Jala Bhedaḥ*, it is not known when, where, or for whom this work by Shri Vallabh was written. It describes the various listeners of the paths of devotion (*bhakti*) and surrender (*prapatti*). The types of listeners are as follows:

Uttamādhikārī—the most exalted bhakti listeners are fully renounced from worldly and Vedic activities, totally attracted to Bhagavan, and their hearts and minds are fully immersed in Krishna nectar.

Madhyamādhikārī—the middling level bhakti listeners focus primarily on the meaning of the teachings they hear. They are overcome with the nectar of devotion only while listening to sacred subjects. Because they have faith only in the reward of listening to kathā, they are not constantly overcome with the nectar of devotion.

Kaniṣṭhādhikārī—The lowest level of bhakti listeners focus mainly on the words of the kathā and are filled with devotional nectar only at the time of listening. Otherwise they are attracted to other things.

Lastly, the best listeners on the path of surrender are those who, by means of the six limbs of dharma (location, time, wealth, agency, mantra, and karma), leave all other unrelated refuge and take the one-pointed shelter of Bhagavan alone.

Saṃnyāsa Nirṇayaḥ

In this text Shri Acharya-charana instructs that, especially in this age of Kali Yuga, sannyasa (renunciation) in the sense intended in the path of *karma* is prohibited. In the paths of *bhakti* and *jñāna* (wisdom), however, there are various accepted methods of taking sannyasa.

Renunciation in the path of wisdom is of two types: *vividiṣā saṃnyāsa* and *vidvat saṃnyāsa*: renunciation by those who aspire towards knowledge, and by those who posess knowledge. The first type is practiced in order to attain wisdom, and the latter is done after wisdom arises.

Bhakti renunciation is also of two types: the first is undergone as a means (*sādhana*) by which listening and other bhakti practices can be well performed. The second type of bhakti renunciation is not a means but rather a reward; it is done in order to experience separation from Bhagavan.

The first of these two types, taking renunciation as a means, is not recommended, because continuously maintaining listening and other bhakti practices requires keeping the company of others, which is contrary to the dharma of sannyasa. Due to the current Kali Yuga and all its impurities, one who renounces as a means is likely to become attracted to worldly activities and become a hypocrite. That is why in the bhakti path, renunciation as a sadhana is not beneficial, whereas renunciation for the purpose of experiencing separation from Bhagavan is praiseworthy. These are the instructions given by Shri Acharyaji in *Saṃnyāsa Nirṇayaḥ*.

Nirodha Lakṣaṇam

Shri Vallabh explains in this text that the distinguishing feature of nirodha is complete forgetfulness of the mundane world, followed by attraction to Bhagavan. The implication (*lakṣaṇa*) in terms of form (*svarūpa*) is as above: forgetfulness of the mundane (*prapañca*) and attraction to Prabhu. The implied effect (*kārya*) of Bhagavad nirodha is the experience of supreme bliss in union with Bhagavan and intense separation at all other times. The implied cause (*kāraṇa*) of nirodha is supreme Brahman, with all his full powers pervading this earth, because it is through Bhagavan's plays here on earth that bhaktas are able to forget the mundane world and become attracted to him. Or, the implied cause is simply becoming immersed and constrained in the Lord's plays. Lastly, in terms of the implied purpose (*prayojana*) of nirodha, it is declared in this text that there is no mantra, prayer, knowledge, nor place of pilgrimage superior to the state of Bhagavad nirodha; it is superior to all else.

Sevā Phalam

It is said that Shri Mahaprabhuji originally composed the *Sevā Phalam* text for one of his *sevaks* (disciples) named Vishnudas Chipa, but because of the difficulty of this text, Vishnudasji was unable to comprehend it. At his request, Shri Acharyaji, through his grace, composed a commentary called *Sevā Phala Vivaraṇam*, to further illuminate the teachings. This is the only one of the *16 Works* for which Shri Acharyaji composed his own commentary.

The essence of *Sevā Phalam* is that there are three rewards to be experienced in seva: *alaukika sāmarthya*, the power to experience divinity; *sāyujya*, union; and attaining a body useful for seva in Vaikuntha and other divine realms. There are also three hindrances to seva: anxiety (*udvega*), which is to be relinquished; worldly enjoyment (*bhoga*), which should be given up, as it is obstructive, destructive and fleeting (divine enjoyment, on the other hand, is a divine reward and should not be relinquished); and obstructions (*pratibandha*), which are also of two types: ordinary and those created by Bhagavan. Ordinary obstructions can be overcome through clever reasoning. Divinely created obstructions cannot be overcome. We do not have the power to do so, so Shri Acharyaji teaches that they should be withstood and supplanted with seva, katha, kirtan, etc. These are the teachings that can be understood by studying Shrimad Acharya-charana's *Sevā Phalam* text and its *Vivaraṇam* commentary.

—Goswami Shri Prabhuji
(Milan Kumar) Mahodaya

NOTES

1 Shri Vitthalnathji, *Śrī Sarvottama Stotram, The Best Recitation*: 13

2 *The Best Recitation*: 11

3 The word *"caraṇa"* (feet) is often affixed to the names of these great teachers, in the tradition of honoring the feet of elders and gurus.

4 *śāstram-avagatya mano-vāg-dehaiḥ kṛṣṇaḥ sevyaḥ* (Shri Vallabhacharya, *Tattvārtha Dīpa Nibandha* 1.4)

5 *evaṁ ṣoḍaśabhir-granthaiḥ puruṣottama-sevanam* (Shri Dvarkesh, *Anvayabodhinī*)

Editor's Note

One intention for this edition was to facilitate the recitation of the original Sanskrit works so brilliantly translated into English here by Shyamdas. To that end I have divided large Sanskrit compounds where possible while keeping sandhi intact. Hyphens have been inserted where compound division rendered a final vowel. For division of compounds, I have relied heavily on the *Puṣṭividhānam* publications, edited by the erudite Pushtimarg lineage holder Goswami Shyam Monohar, which deconstruct sandhi and provide word for word meaning (*anvayārtha*).[1] The Sanskrit text presented here primarily follows the excellent work of the editors Mulchand Telivala and Dhairyalal Sankalia, who in the 1920s collected and published the traditional commentaries on each of Shri Vallabhacharya's *16 Works.*[2]

We have appended to this edition the text *Lover's Life,* certainly one of Shyamdasji's most valuable contributions to English literature on the Pushtimarg. *Lover's Life* is his commentary on *Viveka Dhairyāśrayaḥ* (*Wisdom, Perseverance, and Refuge*), the 8th of Vallabhacharya's *16 Works* as presented in this collection. In this innovative work, Shyamdas draws from traditional Sanskrit commentaries on *Viveka Dhairyāśrayaḥ* to reveal the devotional empowerments both conveyed in the original work and further illuminated by Pushti commentators over the centuries. An enormously helpful guide to unlock the meaning and contemporary relevance of Shri Vallabhacharya's teachings, *Lover's Life* was previously published as an independent book (in some printings under the title *Loving Wisdom*) and is also now available as an audio book read by Shyamdas himself.

My heartfelt appreciation and "Jai Shri Krishna!" to Prakash Pathsariya—who painstakingly transcribed the initial draft of the devanagari text for this edition—and to Shyamdasji's niece Mae Ryan, whose generous financial support made possible the exacting preparation of this 3rd edition.

It is bittersweet to publish this book now without the physical presence of my mentor and friend Shyamdas. His legacy of scholarship, teachings, kirtan, dedication to the path of grace, and most of all, *bhāva,* continues to deeply inspire.

—Vallabhdas

NOTES

1 *Puṣṭividhānam: Vrajabhāṣā Vivecana.* Shri Vallabhacharya Trust, Mandavi-Kutch: V.S. 2069 (2005 CE).
Puṣṭividhānam: Pāṭhāvalī. Edited by Goswami Shyam Manohar. Self published, V.S. 2052 (1995 CE).

2 *Ṣoḍaśagranthāḥ. Edited by Mulcand Telivala and Dhairyalal Sankalia.* Nirnaya Sagara Press, Mumbai, 1921-1925.

Introduction

This collection contains many of the important writings of Shri Vallabhacharya (1479–1531 CE), the founding acharya of the Pushtimarg, the path of grace, and proponent of the purely non-dual philosophy of Shuddhadvaita Vedanta. His *16 Works (Ṣoḍaśa-Granthāḥ)* are presented here in Sanskrit with original English translations, along with a few introductory verses by other authors and two additional works by Shri Vallabhacharya. To read or recite these texts is the most direct approach to understanding Shri Vallabhacharya's path of grace. These short doctrines give a comprehensive view of the path of grace from both philosophical and devotional perspectives.

Siddhānta is true philosophy—teachings that bring us to perfection. It is perfection (*siddha*) at the end (*anta*). Shri Vallabhacharya's siddhanta is strictly for the attainment of Shri Krishna and is full of devotional, inspirational, and practical advice for his followers. His words are replete with wisdom and love and are essential *bhakti* (devotional) empowerments. The blessed master's teachings nurture the delicate inner seed of devotion and guard it from the confusion and false identifications that can cloud our vision and make us forget our true blissful nature. This seed of devotion begins as a subtle notion and can mature into a wishing tree that provides the blessed one with the priceless fruit of bhakti—supreme, unconditional devotion. In that blessed state, the Beloved appears in the heart and throughout creation, filling us with his own joy. This is my humble attempt to present the master's teachings, and any imperfections in the translation are purely my own.

—Shyamdas
2010

मङ्गलाचरणम्

Maṅgalācaraṇam

Auspicious Beginning

These passages are the first to be recited in the morning. They pay homage to Shri Vallabhacharya, his son Shri Gusainji, and Shri Gusainji's seven sons. These prayers remember the main forms of Shri Krishna worshipped in the path of grace, as well as the tenth canto of the *Shrimad Bhagavatam*, Shri Yamunaji, and Shri Girirajji. Bowing before one's guru and God are the main devotional practices.

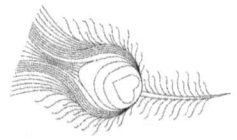

चिन्ता-सन्तान-हन्तारो यत्पादाम्बुज-रेणवः ।
स्वीयानां तान् निजाचार्यान् प्रणमामि मुहुर् मुहुः ॥१॥

cintā-santāna-hantāro yatpādāmbuja-reṇavaḥ
1 *svīyānāṃ tān nijācāryān praṇamāmi muhur muhuḥ*

यद् अनुग्रहतो जन्तुः सर्वदुःखातिगो भवेत् ।
तमहं सर्वदा वन्दे श्रीमद् वल्लभ-नन्दनम् ॥२॥

yad anugrahato jantuḥ sarvaduḥkhātigo bhavet
2 *tamahaṃ sarvadā vande śrīmad vallabha-nandanam*

अज्ञान-तिमिरान्धस्य ज्ञानाञ्जन-शलाकया ।
चक्षुर् उन्मीलितं येन तस्मै श्रीगुरवे नमः ॥३॥

ajñāna-timirāndhasya jñānāñjana-śalākayā
3 *cakṣur unmīlitaṃ yena tasmai śrīgurave namaḥ*

नमामि हृदये शेषे लीला-क्षीराब्धि-शायिनम् ।
लक्ष्मी-सहस्र-लीलाभिः सेव्यमानं कलानिधिम् ॥४॥

namāmi hṛdaye śeṣe līlā-kṣīrābdhi-śāyinam
4 *lakṣmī-sahasra-līlābhiḥ sevyamānaṃ kalānidhim*

चतुर्भिश्च चतुर्भिश्च चतुर्भिश्च त्रिभिस्तथा ।
षड्भिर् विराजते योऽसौ पञ्चधा हृदये मम ॥५॥

caturbhiśca caturbhiśca caturbhiśca tribhistathā
5 *ṣaḍbhir virājate yo'sau pañcadhā hṛdaye mama*

I bow again and again to my teacher,
Shrimad Vallabhacharya.
The dust from his lotus feet
removes all anxieties from his disciples. 1

I always bow to the feet
of Shri Vallabhacharya's son Shri Vitthalnathji.
With his grace, all the woes of the people are removed. 2

I bow to the guru who has applied
the khol of knowledge to my eyes and
thus removed the darkness of ignorance. 3

I bow to Shri Krishna,
an ocean of divine potency
who is served by thousands of Lakshmis
all engaged in his lila (divine play).
They all rest within the limitless heart
that contains the milky nectarine ocean of lila. 4

I bow to the five parts of the *Shrimad Bhagavatam's* 10th canto.
They are the four chapters of Shri Krishna's birth,
the four chapters of his tamas lila,
the four chapters of his rajas lila,
the three chapters of his sattvic lila,
and the six chapters that reveal his divine virtues. 5

श्रीगोवर्धन-नाथ-पाद-युगलं हैयङ्गवीन-प्रियम्।
नित्यं श्रीमथुराधिपं सुखकरं श्रीविट्ठलेशं मुदा।
श्रीमद् द्वारवतीश गोकुलपतिं श्रीगोकुलेन्दुं विभुं।
श्रीमन्मन्मथ-मोहनं नटवरं श्रीबालकृष्णं भजेत्॥६॥

śrīgovardhana-nātha-pāda-yugalaṃ haiyaṅgavīna-priyam
nityaṃ śrīmathurādhipaṃ sukhakaraṃ śrīviṭṭhaleśaṃ mudā
śrīmad dvāravatīśa gokulapatiṃ śrīgokulenduṃ vibhuṃ
6 *śrīmanmanmatha-mohanaṃ naṭavaraṃ śrībālakṛṣṇaṃ bhajet*

श्रीमद् वल्लभ-विट्ठलौ गिरिधरं गोविन्दरायाभिधं।
श्रीमद्बालकृष्ण-गोकुलपती नाथं रघूणांस्तथा॥
एवं श्रीयदुनायकं किल घनश्यामं च तद् वंशजान्।
कालिन्दीं स्वगुरुं गिरिं गुरुविभुं स्वीय-प्रभूंश्च स्मरेत्॥७॥

śrīmad vallabha-viṭṭhalau giridharaṃ govindarāyābhidhaṃ
śrīmadbālakṛṣṇa-gokulapatī nāthaṃ raghūṇāṃstathā
evaṃ śrīyadunāyakaṃ kila ghanaśyāmaṃ ca tad vaṃśajān
7 *kālindīṃ svaguruṃ giriṃ guruvibhuṃ svīya-prabhūṃśca smaret*

Worship Shri Govardhana Nathji's lotus feet
and young Navanita Priyaji, who loves fresh butter.
Worship eternal Shri Mathuradheesh, giver of pleasure,
and the ever-pleased Shri Vitthalesh.
Adore Shri Dwarkadheesh,
Shri Gokulnathji, the Lord of Gokul,
and Shri Gokul Chandramaji, the Moon of Gokul.
Worship Madan Mohanji, the enchanter of even Cupid.
Worship Shri Natavara Prabhu, dancing Child Krishna,
the supreme actor and lover,
and the divine infant Shri Bala Krishna. 6

Remember Shri Vallabhacharya, his son Shri Vitthalnathji,
as well as Shri Vitthalnathji's seven sons:
Shri Giridhar, Shri Govinda,
Shri Balakrishna, Shri Gokulanath,
Shri Raghunath, Shri Yadunath, and Shri Ghanashyam.
Remember their lineages, Shri Yamunaji,
your own guru, the blessed mountain Giriraj,
as well as the Krishna your guru worships.
Remember your own Krishna, the one you serve. 7

श्रीकृष्णस्वरूपध्यानम्

Śrī Kṛṣṇa Svarūpa Dhyānam

बर्हापीडं नटवरवपुः कर्णयोः कर्णिकारं।
बिभ्रद् वासः कनककपिशं वैजयन्तीं च मालां॥
रन्ध्रान् वेणोर् अधर-सुधया पूरयन् गोप-वृन्दैः।
वृन्दारण्यं स्वपद-रमणं प्राविशद् गीतकीर्तिः॥

barhāpīḍaṃ naṭavaravapuḥ karṇayoḥ karṇikāraṃ
bibhrad vāsaḥ kanakakapiśaṃ vaijayantīṃ ca mālāṃ
randhrān veṇor adhara-sudhayā pūrayan gopa-vṛndaiḥ
vṛndāraṇyaṃ svapada-ramaṇaṃ prāviśad gītakīrtiḥ

Shri Krishna's Form

This passage is from the Shrimad Bhagavatam, *in the chapter called the* Venu Gita, *the song of Shri Krishna's flute:*

Shri Krishna is adorned with a peacock feather,
and his ears are graced with flowers.
His shawl is the color of brilliant gold.
He wears a garland made of forest flowers
and appears as the actor-husband.
He is the svaminis' choice, their Lord and husband.
He fills the holes of his flute
with the nectar from his lips.
His praises are sung as he enters Vrindavan,
surrounded by his cowlad friends.
His lotus feet appear splendid and create dalliance
wherever they touch the earth.

श्रीमदाचार्यचरणस्वरूपध्यानम्

Śrīmad Ācāryacaraṇa Svarūpa Dhyānam

सौन्दर्यं निजहृद्गतं प्रकटितं स्त्री-गूढ-भावात्मकं ।
पुंरूपञ्च पुनस्तदन्तरगतं प्रावीविशत् स्वप्रिये ॥
संश्लिष्टावुभयोर्-बभौ रसमयः कृष्णो हि यत् साक्षिकं ।
रूपं तत् त्रितयात्मकं परमभिध्येयं सदा वल्लभम् ॥

saundaryaṃ nijahṛdgataṃ prakaṭitaṃ strī-gūḍha-bhāvātmakaṃ
puṃrūpañca punastadantaragataṃ prāvīviśat svapriye
saṃśliṣṭāvubhayor-babhau rasamayaḥ kṛṣṇo hi yat sākṣikaṃ
rūpaṃ tat tritayātmakaṃ paramabhidhyeyaṃ sadā vallabham

Shri Vallabhacharya's Form

This composition reveals the lila form of Shri Vallabhacharya:

Shri Krishna manifested from his own heart
an exceedingly lovely form of
Shri Svamini's secret and loving feminine mood.
Then, Shri Svamini manifested the all-attractive
male form of Shri Krishna from her heart.
These two forms then entered
their beloved Vallabhacharya and made him
not only a nectar-filled combination of
both divine forms, but their witness as well.
Always contemplate this magnificent,
three-fold form of beloved Shrimad Vallabhacharya.

श्रीविट्ठलनाथप्रभुचरणध्यानम्
Śrīviṭṭhalanātha Prabhucaraṇa Dhyānam

सायं कुञ्जालयस्थासनमुपविलसत् स्वर्णपात्रं सुधौतं।
राजद् यज्ञोपवीतं परितनुवसनं गौरमम्भोज-वक्त्रम्॥
प्राणानायम्य नासा-पुट-निहित-करं कर्ण-राजद् विमुक्तं।
वन्देऽर्धोन्मीलिताक्षं मृगमद-तिलकं विट्ठलेशं सुकेशम्॥

sāyaṃ kuñjālayasthāsanam-upavilasat
svarṇapātraṃ sudhautaṃ
rājad yajñopavītaṃ paritanuvasanaṃ
gauramambhoja-vaktram
prāṇānāyamya nāsā-puṭa-nihita-karaṃ
karṇa-rājad vimuktaṃ
vande'rdhonmīlitākṣaṃ mṛgamada-tilakaṃ
viṭṭhaleśaṃ sukeśam

॥इति मङ्गलाचरणं सम्पूर्णम्॥

iti maṅgalācaraṇaṃ sampūrṇam

Shri Vitthalnathji's Form

Bow to Shri Vitthalnathji, son of Shri Vallabhacharya,
who sits in a lovely bower at sunset.
In front of him are shining golden vessels
for his sandhya prayers.
He is wearing a sacred thread,
a delicate cotton dhoti, and a shawl.
His face shines like a lotus
as he controls his breath by performing pranayama,
placing the fingers of his right hand on his nose.
His ears are adorned with pearl earrings,
and his eyes are half closed.
His forehead is adorned with a musk tilak
and lovely locks of hair.

Thus concludes the Maṅgalācaraṇam.

श्री सर्वोत्तमस्तोत्रम्

Śrī Sarvottama Stotram

The Best Recitation

These verses featuring Shri Vallabhacharya's 108 names, composed by his son Shri Vitthalnathji (Shri Gusainji), contain the heart of the path of grace. These blessed names, recited daily by Shri Vallabhacharya's followers, are the keys to Shri Krishna's grace filled realm. The names speak for themselves.

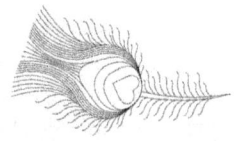

प्राकृत-धर्मानाश्रयम् अप्राकृत-निखिल-धर्मरूपम् इति ।
निगमप्रतिपाद्यं यत् तच्छुद्धं साकृति स्तौमि ॥१॥

prākṛta-dharmānāśrayam aprākṛta-nikhila-dharmarūpam iti
1 *nigamapratipādyaṃ yat tacchuddhaṃ sākṛti staumi*

कलिकाल-तमश्छन्न-दृष्टित्वाद् विदुषामपि ।
सम्प्रत्यविषयस् तस्य माहात्म्यं समभूद् भुवि ॥२॥

kalikāla-tamaśchanna-dṛṣṭitvād viduṣāmapi
2 *sampratyaviṣayas tasya māhātmyaṃ samabhūd bhuvi*

दयया निजमाहात्म्यं करिष्यन् प्रकटं हरिः ।
वाण्या यदा तदा स्वास्यं प्रादुर्भूतं चकार हि ॥३॥

dayayā nijamāhātmyaṃ kariṣyan prakaṭaṃ hariḥ
3 *vāṇyā yadā tadā svāsyaṃ prādurbhūtaṃ cakāra hi*

तदुक्तमपि दुर्बोधं सुबोधं स्याद् यथा तथा ।
तन्नामाष्टोत्तरशतं प्रवक्ष्याम्यखिलाघहृत् ॥४॥

taduktamapi durbodhaṃ subodhaṃ syād yathā tathā
4 *tannāmāṣṭottaraśataṃ pravakṣyāmyakhilāghahṛt*

ऋषिर् अग्निकुमारस्तु नाम्नां छन्दो जगत्यसौ ।
श्रीकृष्णास्यं देवता च बीजं कारुणिकः प्रभुः ॥५॥

ṛṣir agnikumārastu nāmnāṃ chando jagatyasau
5 *śrīkṛṣṇāsyaṃ devatā ca bījaṃ kāruṇikaḥ prabhuḥ*

The manifested form of supreme Brahman
does not rely on any material attributes;
he is full of only divine virtues.
I praise this supreme Brahman
who is, as the Vedas declare,
pure and manifested with form. 1

During this current age of struggle,
the vision of even intelligent people
has been obscured by darkness,
and the greatness of the blessed Lord's form
has not dawned on them. 2

When Shri Hari (Shri Krishna)
became full of compassion
and wanted to manifest
his own greatness through his speech,
his own face appeared as Shri Vallabhacharya. 3

Although what Shri Vallabhacharya taught
is difficult to understand,
through the 108 names I am going to recite,
his words will become easily comprehensible,
and all impurities will be removed. 4

I am the son of the Fire Rishi, Shri Vallabhacharya.
These names are recited
in the well known Anustupa meter,
which has sixteen syllables per line.
In this devotional composition,
Shri Krishna's compassion is the seed,
and his face is the deity. 5

विनियोगो भक्तियोग-प्रतिबन्ध-विनाशने ।
कृष्णाधरामृतास्वाद-सिद्धिर् अत्र न संशयः ॥ ६॥

viniyogo bhaktiyoga-pratibandha-vināśane
6 *kṛṣṇādharāmṛtāsvāda-siddhir atra na saṃśayaḥ*

आनन्दः परमानन्दः श्रीकृष्णास्यं कृपानिधिः ।
दैवोद्धार-प्रयत्नात्मा स्मृतिमात्रार्तिनाशनः ॥ ७॥

ānandaḥ paramānandaḥ śrīkṛṣṇāsyaṃ kṛpānidhiḥ
7 *daivoddhāra-prayatnātmā smṛtimātrārtināśanaḥ*

श्रीभागवत-गूढार्थ-प्रकाशन-परायणः ।
साकार-ब्रह्म-वादैक-स्थापको वेदपारगः ॥ ८॥

śrībhāgavata-gūḍhārtha-prakāśana-parāyaṇaḥ
8 *sākāra-brahma-vādaika-sthāpako vedapāragaḥ*

मायावाद-निराकर्ता सर्ववादि-निरासकृत् ।
भक्तिमार्गाब्जमार्तण्डः स्त्रीशूद्राद्युद्धृतिक्ष्मः ॥ ९॥

māyāvāda-nirākartā sarvavādi-nirāsakṛt
9 *bhaktimārgābjamārtaṇḍaḥ strīśūdrādyuddhṛtikṣmaḥ*

अङ्गीकृत्यैव गोपीश-वल्लभी-कृत-मानवः ।
अङ्गीकृतौ समर्यादो महाकारुणिको विभुः ॥ १०॥

aṅgīkṛtyaiva gopīśa-vallabhī-kṛta-mānavaḥ
10 *aṅgīkṛtau samaryādo mahākāruṇiko vibhuḥ*

These 108 names are useful in the practice of bhakti yoga.
By reciting them, one's obstructions will be removed
and without a doubt, one will receive the reward of
the nectar of Shri Krishna's lips. 6

[Here begin the sacred names:]

Shri Vallabhacharya is full of bliss—supreme bliss.
He is the form of Shri Krishna's face and an ocean of grace.
He is soulfully intent upon uplifting divine souls.
Afflictions are removed by simply remembering him. 7

Shri Vallabhacharya is intent upon revealing
the esoteric meanings of the *Shrimad Bhagavatam*.
He established the truth that Brahman has a divine form,
and he is the knower of the inner Veda. 8

He defeated the theories which state
that the world is comprised of illusory *maya*,
and he dispelled the confusion of all other false teachings.
For the lotus-like path of devotion,
Shri Vallabhacharya is the sun.
He uplifts women, the low caste, and others. 9

Those souls whom he accepted
became beloved to Shri Krishna, the Lord of the gopis.
Shri Vallabhacharya initiated souls
in accordance with scriptural law.
He is extremely compassionate and all-powerful. 10

अदेय-दान-दक्षश्च महोदार-चरित्रवान्।
प्राकृतानुकृति-व्याज-मोहितासुर-मानुषः ॥११॥

adeya-dāna-dakṣaśca mahodāra-caritravān
11 *prākṛtānukṛti-vyāja-mohitāsura-mānuṣaḥ*

वैश्वानरो वल्लभाख्यः सद्रूपो हितकृत् सताम्।
जनशिक्षाकृते कृष्ण-भक्तिकृद् निखिलेष्टदः ॥१२॥

vaiśvānaro vallabhākhyaḥ sadrūpo hitakṛt satām
12 *janaśikṣākṛte kṛṣṇa-bhaktikṛd nikhileṣṭadaḥ*

सर्व-लक्षण-सम्पन्नः श्रीकृष्ण-ज्ञानदो गुरुः।
स्वानन्द-तुन्दिलः पद्म-दलायत-विलोचनः ॥१३॥

sarva-lakṣaṇa-sampannaḥ śrīkṛṣṇa-jñānado guruḥ
13 *svānanda-tundilaḥ padma-dalāyata-vilocanaḥ*

कृपा-दृग् वृष्टि-संहृष्ट-दास-दासी-प्रियः पतिः।
रोष-दृक् पात-सम्प्लुष्ट-भक्तद्विट् भक्तसेवितः ॥१४॥

kṛpā-dṛg vṛṣṭi-saṃhṛṣṭa-dāsa-dāsī-priyaḥ patiḥ
14 *roṣa-dṛk pāta-sampluṣṭa-bhaktadviṭ bhaktasevitaḥ*

सुखसेव्यो दुराराध्यो दुर्लभाङ्घ्रि-सरोरुहः।
उग्रप्रतापो वाक्सीधु-पूरिताशेष-सेवकः ॥१५॥

sukhasevyo durārādhyo durlabhāṅghri-saroruhaḥ
15 *ugrapratapo vāksīdhu-pūritāśeṣa-sevakaḥ*

Shri Vallabhacharya is brilliant at giving the ungivable,
and his character is full of generosity.
He deluded ungodly souls
by appearing to them as an ordinary man. 11

Shri Vallabhacharya is the God of Fire
and is known as the Beloved.
His form is pure and beneficial to the saints.
In order to teach others, he himself
practiced Krishna bhakti and fulfilled all desires. 12

Shri Vallabhacharya is full of all divine virtues
and gives understanding of Shri Krishna.
Shri Vallabhacharya is the guru.
He is satisfied in his own bliss,
and his eyes are wide like lotus flowers. 13

Shri Vallabhacharya's beloved male and female followers
are delighted by his grace filled glance.
He is the master.
His fierce glance incinerates the bhaktas' enemies.
He is served by the bhaktas. 14

Shri Vallabhacharya's worship is pleasurable
and difficult to attain for those who are not bhaktas.
It is very rare to attain his lotus feet.
He is extremely powerful,
and his nectar-like speech fills all of his disciples. 15

श्रीभागवत-पीयूष-समुद्र-मथन-क्षमः ।
तत्सारभूत-रासस्त्रीभाव-पूरित-विग्रहः ॥१६॥

śrībhāgavata-pīyūṣa-samudra-mathana-kṣamaḥ
16 *tatsārabhūta-rāsastrībhāva-pūrita-vigrahaḥ*

सान्निध्य-मात्र-दत्त-श्रीकृष्णप्रेमा विमुक्तिदः ।
रासलीलैक-तात्पर्यः कृपयैतत्कथा-प्रदः ॥१७॥

sānnidhya-mātra-datta-śrīkṛṣṇapremā vimuktidaḥ
17 *rāsalīlaika-tātparyaḥ kṛpayaitatkathā-pradaḥ*

विरहानुभवैकार्थ-सर्व-त्यागोपदेशकः ।
भक्त्याचारोपदेष्टा च कर्म-मार्ग-प्रवर्तकः ॥१८॥

virahānubhavaikārtha-sarva-tyāgopadeśakaḥ
18 *bhaktyācāropadeṣṭā ca karma-mārga-pravartakaḥ*

यागादौ भक्तिमार्गैक-साधनत्वोपदेशकः ।
पूर्णानन्दः पूर्णकामो वाक्पतिर् विबुधेश्वरः ॥१९॥

yāgādau bhaktimārgaika-sādhanatvopadeśakaḥ
19 *pūrṇānandaḥ pūrṇakāmo vākpatir vibudheśvaraḥ*

कृष्ण-नाम-सहस्रस्य वक्ता भक्तपरायणः ।
भक्त्याचारोपदेशार्थ-नाना-वाक्य-निरूपकः ॥२०॥

kṛṣṇa-nāma-sahasrasya vaktā bhaktaparāyaṇaḥ
20 *bhaktyācāropadeśārtha-nānā-vākya-nirūpakaḥ*

Shri Vallabhacharya churned
the nectarine ocean of the *Shrimad Bhagavatam*.
His form brims with the *bhāva* (devotional mood)
of the gopis dancing the Rasa Lila with Shri Krishna. 16

By Shri Vallabhacharya's mere proximity,
love for Shri Krishna is attained.
He gives grace filled liberation.
His essential message is the Rasa Lila,
and by his grace, he gave his followers
teachings on that divine subject. 17

Shri Vallabhacharya teaches that in order to experience
the blissful pangs of separation from Shri Krishna,
everything else has to be renounced.
He gave teachings on the path of devotion (*bhakti*)
and promoted the path of action (*karma mārga*) as well. 18

Shri Vallabhacharya teaches that
sacrifices and other Vedic practices
can all play a part in the path of devotion.
Shri Vallabhacharya is full of bliss,
and his every desire is fulfilled.
He is the master of speech and the Lord of the wise. 19

Shri Vallabhacharya spoke the thousand names of Shri Krishna.
He focuses on his followers. Shri Vallabhacharya
spoke and wrote about many different subjects
in order to teach the path of devotion. 20

स्वार्थोज्झिताखिल-प्राण-प्रियस् तादृश-वेष्टितः ।
स्वदासार्थ-कृताशेष-साधनः सर्वशक्तिधृक् ॥२१॥

svārthojjhitākhila-prāṇa-priyas tādṛśa-veṣṭitaḥ
21 *svadāsārtha-kṛtāśeṣa-sādhanaḥ sarvaśaktidhṛk*

भुवि भक्ति-प्रचारैक-कृते स्वान्वयकृत् पिता ।
स्ववंशे स्थापिताशेष-स्वमाहात्म्यः स्मयापहः ॥२२॥

bhuvi bhakti-pracāraika-kṛte svānvayakṛt pitā
22 *svavaṃśe sthāpitāśeṣa-svamāhātmyaḥ smayāpahaḥ*

पति-व्रता-पतिः पारलौकिकैहिक-दानकृत् ।
निगूढ-हृदयोऽनन्य-भक्तेषु ज्ञापिताशयः ॥२३॥

pati-vratā-patiḥ pāralaukikaihika-dānakṛt
23 *nigūḍha-hṛdayo'nanya-bhakteṣu jñāpitāśayaḥ*

उपासनादि-मार्गाति-मुग्ध-मोह-निवारकः ।
भक्तिमार्गे सर्वमार्ग-वैलक्षण्यानुभूतिकृत् ॥२४॥

upāsanādi-mārgāti-mugdha-moha-nivārakaḥ
24 *bhaktimārge sarvamārga-vailakṣaṇyānubhūtikṛt*

पृथक् शरणमार्गोपदेष्टा श्रीकृष्ण-हार्दवित् ।
प्रतिक्षण-निकुञ्जस्थ-लीला-रस-सुपूरितः ॥२५॥

pṛthak śaraṇamārgopadeṣṭā śrīkṛṣṇa-hārdavit
25 *pratikṣaṇa-nikuñjastha-līlā-rasa-supūritaḥ*

To uplift his followers, Shri Vallabhacharya
renounced everything unrelated to devotion.
He is surrounded by accomplished souls and has
performed all sorts of practices for his dear followers.
Shri Vallabhacharya contains every power. 21

Shri Vallabhacharya created his own family lineage
in order to promote devotion in the world.
He is a father and has established
his unlimited greatness in his own lineage.
He is the remover of pride. 22

Shri Vallabhacharya is the husband to those who are
devoted to the eternal husband, Shri Krishna.
He is a giver of divine and worldly gifts.
His heart is very esoteric,
but he reveals his inner intentions
to his one-pointed devotees. 23

Shri Vallabhacharya removes the confusion
of those bewildered by the various paths of practice.
He gave his followers the experience of how
the path of devotion is distinct from all other paths. 24

Shri Vallabhacharya teaches
a distinct path of refuge (*śaraṇa mārga*).
He is the knower of Shri Krishna's inner essence
and is always filled with the nectar
of Shri Krishna's bower lilas. 25

तत् कथाक्षिप्त-चित्तस् तद् विस्मृतान्यो व्रजप्रियः ।
प्रिय-व्रज-स्थितिः पुष्टि-लीला-कर्ता रहःप्रियः ॥२६॥

tat kathākṣipta-cittas tad vismṛtānyo vrajapriyaḥ
26 *priya-vraja-sthitiḥ pusṭi-līlā-kartā rahaḥpriyaḥ*

भक्तेच्छा-पूरकः सर्वा-ज्ञातलीलोऽति-मोहनः ।
सर्वासक्तो भक्त-मात्रासक्तः पतित-पावनः ॥२७॥

bhaktecchā-pūrakaḥ sarvā-jñātalīlo'ti-mohanaḥ
27 *sarvāsakto bhakta-mātrāsaktaḥ patita-pāvanaḥ*

स्वयशो-गान-संहृष्ट-हृदयाम्भोज-विष्टरः ।
यशःपीयूष-लहरी-प्लावितान्य-रसः परः ॥२८॥

svayaśo-gāna-saṃhṛṣṭa-hṛdayāmbhoja-viṣṭaraḥ
28 *yaśaḥpīyūṣa-laharī-plāvitānya-rasaḥ paraḥ*

लीलामृत-रसार्द्रार्द्री-कृताखिल-शरीर-भृत् ।
गोवर्धन-स्थित्युत्साहस् तल्लीला-प्रेम-पूरितः ॥२९॥

līlāmṛta-rasārdrārdrī-kṛtākhila-śarīra-bhṛt
29 *govardhana-sthityutsāhas tallīlā-prema-pūritaḥ*

His mind is enthralled by stories of Shri Krishna,
and he has forgotten everything else.
Shri Vallabhacharya loves Vraja, Shri Krishna's land of lila.
He loves to live in Vraja.
He creates grace filled lilas and loves solitude. 26

Shri Vallabhacharya fulfills the wishes of his followers.
His lila is unfathomable, and he is extremely enchanting.
He is not attached to anything except his bhaktas.
Shri Vallabhacharya is the purifier of the fallen. 27

Shri Vallabhacharya lives in the lotus hearts of his bhaktas
who are ecstatic with the song of his praise.
The nectar-filled waves of Shri Vallabhacharya's fame
saturate every mood with the elixir of devotion.
He is totally exalted. 28

Shri Vallabhacharya completely soaks the bodies of his bhaktas
with the blissful nectar of Shri Krishna's lilas.
He lives by the Govardhan Hill with great enthusiasm
and is filled with the love of Shri Krishna's lilas. 29

यज्ञ-भोक्ता यज्ञ-कर्ता चतुर्वर्ग-विशारदः ।
सत्य-प्रतिज्ञस् त्रिगुणातीतो नयविशारदः ॥ ३० ॥

yajña-bhoktā yajña-kartā caturvarga-viśāradaḥ
30 *satya-pratijñas triguṇātīto nayaviśāradaḥ*

स्वकीर्तिवर्धनस् तत्त्व-सूत्र-भाष्य-प्रदर्शकः ।
मायावादाख्य-तूलाग्निर् ब्रह्मवाद-निरूपकः ॥ ३१ ॥

svakīrtivardhanas tattva-sūtra-bhāṣya-pradarśakaḥ
31 *māyāvādākhya-tūlāgnir brahmavāda-nirūpakaḥ*

अप्राकृताखिलाकल्प-भूषितः सहज-स्मितः ।
त्रिलोकी-भूषणं भूमि-भाग्यं सहज-सुन्दरः ॥ ३२ ॥

aprākṛtākhilākalpa-bhūṣitaḥ sahaja-smitaḥ
32 *trilokī-bhūṣaṇaṃ bhūmi-bhāgyaṃ sahaja-sundaraḥ*

अशेष-भक्त-सम्प्रार्थ्य-चरणाब्ज-रजोधनः ।
इत्यानन्दनिधेः प्रोक्तं नाम्नामष्टोत्तरं शतम् ॥ ३३ ॥

aśeṣa-bhakta-samprārthya-caraṇābja-rajodhanaḥ
33 *ityānandanidheḥ proktaṃ nāmnāmaṣṭottaraṃ śatam*

Shri Vallabhacharya is the enjoyer and
performer of sacred ceremonies.
He is brilliant at giving the four pursuits of life.
His oath is pure, and he is beyond
the three material qualities of *sattva*, *rajas*, and *tamas*.
He has brilliant judgment. 30

Shri Vallabhacharya increased his own fame and
wrote a commentary on the *Brahma Sutras*.
Shri Vallabhacharya is fire to the cotton-like,
false teachings of Mayavada.
He has explained the teachings of Brahmavada,
wherein everything is Krishna and nothing but Krishna. 31

Shri Vallabhacharya is adorned with divine ornaments.
He has a natural smile and is the ornament of the three worlds.
He contains the world's fortune and is naturally beautiful. 32

All the bhaktas pray for the dust
that has touched Shri Vallabhacharya's lotus feet.
Thus I have revealed the ocean of bliss,
the 108 names of Shri Vallabhacharya. 33

श्रद्धा-विशुद्ध-बुद्धिर्यः पठत्यनुदिनं जनः ।
स तदेकमनाः सिद्धिम् उक्तां प्राप्नोत्यसंशयम् ॥ ३४॥

śraddhā-viśuddha-buddhiryaḥ paṭhatyanudinaṃ janaḥ
34 *sa tadekamanāḥ siddhim uktāṃ prāpnotyasaṃśayam*

तदप्राप्तौ वृथा मोक्षस् तदाप्तौ तद्गतार्थता ।
अतः सर्वोत्तमं स्तोत्रं जप्यं कृष्ण-रसार्थिभिः ॥ ३५॥

tadaprāptau vṛthā mokṣas tadāptau tadgatārthatā
35 *ataḥ sarvottamaṃ stotraṃ japyaṃ kṛṣṇa-rasārthibhiḥ*

॥इति श्रीमदग्निकुमार-प्रोक्तं सर्वोत्तमस्तोत्रं सम्पूर्णम् ॥
iti śrīmadagnikumāra-proktaṃ sarvottamastotraṃ sampūrṇam

Whoever recites these names of Shri Vallabhacharya
with faith, pure intelligence, and focused mind
will undoubtedly attain
the reward of grace filled Krishna. 34

If the grace filled form of Shri Krishna is not realized,
then even the attainment of liberation is useless.
If Krishna is attained, however,
one is completely accomplished.
And so, recite these praises, which are the best of all,
for the attainment of Shri Krishna, who is pure nectar. 35

Thus ends the Best Recitation, revealed by Shri Gusainji,
son of the Fire Rishi, Shri Vallabhacharya.

श्रीयमुनाष्टकम्

Śrī Yamunāṣṭakam

In Praise of Shri Yamuna

The first of Shri Vallabhacharya's renowned *Sixteen Works* is the *Shri Yamunashtakam*, composed in 1492 CE in the town of Gokul. It is his brilliant praise of the divine Yamuna River, who is also Shri Krishna's most beloved. It is through Shri Yamunaji's grace that one receives the ability to meet Shri Krishna. Yamunaji is the source of all divine powers and increases the bhaktas' love for Shri Krishna. She purifies the earth and removes obstructions that prevent bhaktas from experiencing the blessed Lord. She removes the burdens of this age of struggle, elevates her bhaktas, and makes them dear to Krishna. Finally, she transforms the bhakta and makes her fit for Shri Krishna's loving service. In the master's words...

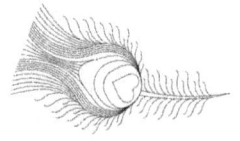

नमामि यमुनामहं सकल-सिद्धि-हेतुं मुदा
मुरारि-पद-पङ्कज-स्फुरदमन्द-रेणूत्कटाम् ॥
तटस्थ-नवकानन-प्रकट-मोद-पुष्पाम्बुना
सुरासुर-सुपूजित-स्मरपितुः श्रियं बिभ्रतीम् ॥ १ ॥

namāmi yamunāmahaṃ sakala-siddhi-hetuṃ mudā
murāri-pada-paṅkaja-sphuradamanda-reṇūtkaṭām
taṭastha-navakānana-prakaṭa-moda-puṣpāmbunā
1 *surāsura-supūjita-smarapituḥ śriyaṃ bibhratīm*

कलिन्द-गिरि-मस्तके पतदमन्द-पूरोज्ज्वला
विलास-गमनोल्लसत् प्रकट-गण्ड-शैलोन्नता ॥
सघोष-गति-दन्तुरा-समधिरूढ-दोलोत्तमा
मुकुन्द-रति-वर्धिनी जयति पद्मबन्धोः सुता ॥ २ ॥

kalinda-giri-mastake patadamanda-pūrojjvalā
vilāsa-gamanollasat prakaṭa-gaṇḍa-śailonnatā
saghoṣa-gati-danturā-samadhirūḍha-dolottamā
2 *mukunda-rati-vardhinī jayati padmabandhoḥ sutā*

भुवं भुवन-पावनीम् अधिगताम् अनेक-स्वनैः
प्रियाभिरिव सेवितां शुक-मयूर-हंसादिभिः ॥
तरङ्ग-भुज-कङ्कण-प्रकट-मुक्तिका-वालुका-
नितम्ब-तट-सुन्दरीं नमत कृष्ण-तुर्य-प्रियाम् ॥ ३ ॥

bhuvaṃ bhuvana-pāvanīm adhigatām aneka-svanaiḥ
priyābhiriva sevitāṃ śuka-mayūra-haṃsādibhiḥ
taraṅga-bhuja-kaṅkaṇa-prakaṭa-muktikā-vālukā-
3 *nitamba-taṭa-sundarīṃ namata kṛṣṇa-turya-priyām*

I joyfully bow to Shri Yamunaji, giver of all divine powers.
Her expansive sands shine brightly,
like the lotus feet of Lord Krishna.
Flowers from fresh forests along Shri Yamunaji's banks
mingle with her and make her waters fragrant.
Both humble and assertive gopis
worship Shri Yamunaji well.
She contains the beauty of Shri Krishna. 1

Shri Yamunaji emerges
from the heart of Lord Narayana,
cascading from the summit of Kalinda Mountain
with brilliance. She appears to be swaying
in a lovely swing as she descends the rocky slopes,
her waters roaring and filled with dalliance.
Glories to Shri Yamunaji, the daughter of the sun,
who increases the bhaktas' love for Mukunda. 2

Shri Yamunaji has come to earth for its purification.
Like the gopis serve their beloved Krishna,
Shri Yamunaji is served by the many songs
of the peacocks, parrots, swans, and other birds.
Her waves are her arms,
and her sands are her pearly bangles.
Her banks are her hips.
Bow to beautiful Yamuna, the fourth and
foremost beloved of Shri Krishna. 3

अनन्त-गुण-भूषिते शिव-विरञ्चि-देव-स्तुते
घनाघन-निभे सदा ध्रुव-पराशराभीष्टदे ॥
विशुद्ध-मथुरा-तटे सकल-गोप-गोपी-वृते
कृपा-जलधि-संश्रिते मम मनः सुखं भावय ॥४॥

ananta-guṇa-bhūṣite śiva-virañci-deva-stute
ghanāghana-nibhe sadā dhruva-parāśarābhīṣṭade
viśuddha-mathurā-taṭe sakala-gopa-gopī-vṛte
4 *kṛpā-jaladhi-saṃśrite mama manaḥ sukhaṃ bhāvaya*

यया चरण-पद्मजा मुररिपोः प्रियम्भावुका
समागमनतोऽभवत् सकल-सिद्धिदा सेवताम् ॥
तया सदृशताम् इयात् कमलजा सपत्नीव यत्
हरि-प्रिय-कलिन्दया मनसि मे सदा स्थीयताम् ॥५॥

yayā caraṇa-padmajā muraripoḥ priyambhāvukā
samāgamanato'bhavat sakala-siddhidā sevatām
tayā sadṛśatām iyāt kamalajā sapatnīva yat
5 *hari-priya-kalindayā manasi me sadā sthīyatām*

नमोऽस्तु यमुने सदा तव चरित्रम् अत्यद्भुतं
न जातु यमयातना भवति ते पयःपानतः ॥
यमोऽपि भगिनी-सुतान् कथमु हन्ति दुष्टानपि
प्रियो भवति सेवनात् तव हरेर् यथा गोपिकाः ॥६॥

namo'stu yamune sadā tava caritram atyadbhutaṃ
na jātu yamayātanā bhavati te payaḥpānataḥ
yamo'pi bhaginī-sutān kathamu hanti duṣṭānapi
6 *priyo bhavati sevanāt tava harer yathā gopikāḥ*

Embellished with countless virtues, Shri Yamunaji is
praised by Shiva, Brahma, and other divinities.
Her hue is always the color of dark clouds.
She fulfilled the wishes of Dhruva and Parasha.
At her banks by the pure city of Mathura,
she is surrounded by the gopis and gopas.
O Yamunaji, you have taken the shelter of
Shri Krishna, the ocean of grace.
Bring joy to my heart. 4

Only after she merged with you, O Yamunaji,
did Ganga become beloved to Shri Krishna.
Only then was Ganga able to give all devotional powers
to those who worship her.
If there is anyone who can even come close to you,
it would be your co-wife, Shri Lakshmi.
May you remain forever in my heart,
Kalindi, beloved of Hari,
destroyer of the strife of this age of Kali. 5

Obeisances to you forever, Shri Yamunaji.
Your story is most amazing.
Those who sip your waters are never tormented
by Yama, the god of retribution,
for how could he ever harm the children
of his younger sister, even if they are bad?
Those who worship you become beloved to Hari,
just like the gopis. 6

ममाऽस्तु तव सन्निधौ तनुनवत्वम् एतावता
न दुर्लभतमा रतिर् मुररिपौ मुकुन्द-प्रिये ॥
अतोऽस्तु तव लालना सुरधुनी परं सङ्गमात्
तवैव भुवि कीर्तिता न तु कदापि पुष्टि-स्थितैः ॥७॥

mamā'stu tava sannidhau tanunavatvam etāvatā
na durlabhatamā ratir muraripau mukunda-priye
ato'stu tava lālanā suradhunī paraṃ saṅgamāt
7 *tavaiva bhuvi kīrtitā na tu kadāpi puṣṭi-sthitaiḥ*

स्तुतिं तव करोति कः कमलजा-सपत्नि प्रिये
हरेर् यद् अनुसेवया भवति सौख्यमामोक्षतः ॥
इयं तव कथाऽधिका सकल-गोपिका-सङ्गम-
स्मर-श्रम-जलाणुभिः सकल-गात्रजैः सङ्गमः ॥८॥

stutiṃ tava karoti kaḥ kamalajā-sapatni priye
harer yad anusevayā bhavati saukhyamāmokṣataḥ
iyaṃ tava kathā'dhikā sakala-gopikā-saṅgama-
8 *smara-śrama-jalāṇubhiḥ sakala-gātrajaiḥ saṅgamaḥ*

तवाऽष्टकम् इदं मुदा पठति सूरसुते सदा-
समस्त-दुरित-क्षयो भवति वै मुकुन्दे रतिः ॥
तया सकल-सिद्धयो मुररिपुश्च सन्तुष्यति
स्वभाव-विजयो भवेद् वदति वल्लभः श्रीहरेः ॥९॥

tavā'ṣṭakam idaṃ mudā paṭhati sūrasute sadā-
samasta-durita-kṣayo bhavati vai mukunde ratiḥ
tayā sakala-siddhayo muraripuśca santuṣyati
9 *svabhāva-vijayo bhaved vadati vallabhaḥ śrīhareḥ*

॥इति श्रीवल्लभाचार्य-विरचितं श्रीयमुनाष्टकं सम्पूर्णम् ॥
iti śrīvallabhācārya-viracitaṃ śrīyamunāṣṭakaṃ sampūrṇam

By being near you, may my body be
divinely transformed and renewed.
Then it will not be difficult at all to love Krishna.
This is why I cherish you.
In this world, grace filled souls
only praise Ganga after she has joined with you. 7

Who is capable of praising you,
Krishna's beloved Shri Yamunaji, co-wife of Lakshmi?
If worshipped together with Shri Hari,
Shri Lakshmi can at best award the bliss of liberation.
Your story, however, is far greater,
for your entire body is composed of
the beads of sweat
that have fallen from Shri Krishna
during his love plays with the gopis. 8

O Yamuna, daughter of the sun!
Those who joyfully recite this eight-fold praise
have all of their impurities removed
and love Shri Krishna, the giver of liberation.
Through you, all devotional powers are attained
and Shri Krishna becomes pleased.
You transform the nature of your bhaktas,
says Shri Vallabhacharya, beloved of Hari. 9

Thus ends Śrī Yamunāṣṭakam by Shri Vallabhacharya.

बालबोधः

Bāla Bodhaḥ

Instructions for Spiritual Children

The next teaching in Shri Vallabhacharya's *Sixteen Works* is *Bāla Bodhaḥ*. He composed this teaching around 1493 CE in Pushkar for his disciple Narayandas. It maps out the different approaches to liberation and is truly a guide for novices on the spiritual path. After explaining four possible ways to achieve liberation, the master touches upon *sevā*, the beloved devotional practice.

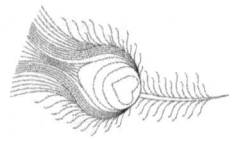

नत्वा हरिं सदानन्दं सर्व-सिद्धान्त-सङ्ग्रहम् ।
बाल-प्रबोधनार्थाय वदामि सुविनिश्चितम् ॥ १॥

natvā hariṃ sadānandaṃ sarva-siddhānta-saṅgraham
1 *bāla-prabodhanārthāya vadāmi suviniścitam*

धर्मार्थ-काम-मोक्षाख्याश् चत्वारोऽर्था मनीषिणाम् ।
जीवेश्वर-विचारेण द्विधा ते हि विचारिताः ॥ २॥

dharmārtha-kāma-mokṣākhyāś catvāro'rthā manīṣiṇām
2 *jīveśvara-vicāreṇa dvidhā te hi vicāritāḥ*

अलौकिकास्तु वेदोक्ताः साध्य-साधन-संयुताः ।
लौकिका ऋषिभिः प्रोक्तास् तथैवेश्वर-शिक्षया ॥ ३॥

alaukikāstu vedoktāḥ sādhya-sādhana-saṃyutāḥ
3 *laukikā ṛṣibhiḥ proktās tathaiveśvara-śikṣayā*

लौकिकांस्तु प्रवक्ष्यामि वेदाद् आद्या यतः स्थिताः ।
धर्म-शास्त्राणि नीतिश्च काम-शास्त्राणि च क्रमात् ॥ ४॥

laukikāṃstu pravakṣyāmi vedād ādyā yataḥ sthitāḥ
4 *dharma-śāstrāṇi nītiśca kāma-śāstrāṇi ca kramāt*

Having bowed to all-blissful Shri Hari,
I will now explain the essence of all teachings
to those souls who are young on the spiritual path. 1

Sages have revealed that
there are four pursuits of human life:
ethical conduct *(dharma)*,
wealth (*artha*),
desire (*kāma*),
and liberation (*mokṣa*).
These teachings have been considered
by teachers in this world,
as well as by God himself. 2

The Vedas have already addressed divine reality
in terms of how to attain it,
as well as the object of that attainment.
The four pursuits of life have also been
proclaimed by sages living in the world,
according to the teachings they received from God. 3

The Vedas have explained divine reality.
I will now explain what the sages
have revealed about the pursuits of life. 4

त्रिवर्ग-साधकानीति न तन्निर्णय उच्यते।
मोक्षे चत्वारि शास्त्राणि लौकिके परतः स्वतः ॥५॥

trivarga-sādhakānīti na tannirṇaya ucyate
5 *mokṣe catvāri śāstrāṇi laukike parataḥ svataḥ*

द्विधा द्वे द्वे स्वतस्तत्र सांख्य-योगौ प्रकीर्तितौ।
त्यागात्याग-विभागेन सांख्ये त्यागः प्रकीर्तितः ॥६॥

dvidhā dve dve svatastatra sāṃkhya-yogau prakīrtitau
6 *tyāgātyāga-vibhāgena sāṃkhye tyāgaḥ prakīrtitaḥ*

अहन्ता-ममता-नाशे सर्वथा निरहङ्कृतौ।
स्वरूपस्थो यदा जीवः कृतार्थः स निगद्यते ॥७॥

ahantā-mamatā-nāśe sarvathā nirahaṅkṛtau
7 *svarūpastho yadā jīvaḥ kṛtārthaḥ sa nigadyate*

तदर्थं प्रक्रिया काचित् पुराणेऽपि निरूपिता।
ऋषिभिर् बहुधा प्रोक्ता फलम् एकम् अबाह्यतः ॥८॥

tadarthaṃ prakriyā kācit purāṇe'pi nirūpitā
8 *ṛṣibhir bahudhā proktā phalam ekam abāhyataḥ*

The doctrines that address dharma, wealth, and erotics
have already detailed the means
to attain those three pursuits of life,
so I will not discuss them here.
There are four traditions concerning
liberation, the fourth pursuit of life.
Two schools teach that
liberation is attained through self effort,
while the other two paths
require taking the assistance of God. 5

Yoga and Sankhya have been mentioned as
the two traditions in which self effort
can produce the liberated state.
The Sankhya system teaches external renunciation,
while the school of eight-fold Yoga
does not promote external renunciation. 6

Practitioners in these two traditions
are deemed spiritually accomplished
when they become forever free
of all mistaken identifications relating to “me and mine.”
Then they become established in their true form. 7

The actual methods for liberation
have been revealed in certain portions of the Puranas.
Enlightened sages have spoken
about liberation in many different ways.
The final reward that they all refer to is the same,
as long as it does not contradict Vedic traditions. 8

अत्यागे योगमार्गो हि त्यागोऽपि मनसैव हि ।
यमादयस्तु कर्तव्याः सिद्धे योगे कृतार्थता ॥ ९ ॥

atyāge yogamārgo hi tyāgo'pi manasaiva hi
9 *yamādayastu kartavyāḥ siddhe yoge kṛtārthatā*

पराश्रयेण मोक्षस्तु द्विधा सोऽपि निरूप्यते ।
ब्रह्मा ब्राह्मणतां यातस् तद्रूपेण सुसेव्यते ॥ १० ॥

parāśrayeṇa mokṣastu dvidhā so'pi nirūpyate
10 *brahmā brāhmaṇatāṃ yātas tadrūpeṇa susevyate*

ते सर्वार्था न चाऽद्येन शास्त्रं किञ्चिद् उदीरितम् ।
अतः शिवश्च विष्णुश्च जगतो हितकारकौ ॥ ११ ॥

te sarvārthā na cā'dyena śāstraṃ kiñcid udīritam
11 *ataḥ śivaśca viṣṇuśca jagato hitakārakau*

वस्तुनः स्थितिसंहारौ कार्यौ शास्त्र-प्रवर्त्तकौ ।
ब्रह्मैव तादृशं यस्मात् सर्वात्मकतयोदितौ ॥ १२ ॥

vastunaḥ sthitisaṃhārau kāryau śāstra-pravarttakau
12 *brahmaiva tādṛśaṃ yasmāt sarvātmakatayoditau*

In the path of Yoga, renunciation is not external,
but is done inwardly with the mind.
The eight-fold practice of knowing
what to do, what to avoid, sitting properly,
breath control, focus, one-pointed concentration,
meditation, and total absorption (*samādhi*)
must all be perfected in this yoga
for the practitioner to become accomplished. 9

The two traditions of liberation which rely on
the help of another (either Vishnu or Shiva)
have also been recognized in Vedic literature.
The creator god, Brahma, is worshipped only
by Brahmins in order for them to perfect
their dharma of being Brahmins. 10
Therefore, Brahma is not resorted to for liberation,
though there are a few mentions of Brahma awarding it.
For those souls who desire to attain liberation
with the help of another, Shiva and Vishnu
are known to be their benefactors in this world. 11

Vishnu is the sustainer of creation, while Shiva is the destroyer.
Both have been revealed as such in their own scriptures.

Know without a doubt that the supreme Brahman
is both Vishnu and Shiva, for they have both been
declared as the self of all things. 12

निर्दोष-पूर्ण-गुणता तत् तच्छास्त्रे तयोः कृता ।
भोगमोक्षफले दातुं शक्तौ द्वावपि यद्यपि ॥१३॥

nirdoṣa-pūrṇa-guṇatā tat tacchāstre tayoḥ kṛtā
13 *bhogamokṣaphale dātuṃ śaktau dvāvapi yadyapi*

भोगः शिवेन मोक्षस्तु विष्णुनेति विनिश्चयः ।
लोकेऽपि यत् प्रभुर्भुंक्ते तन्न यच्छति कर्हिचित् ॥१४॥

bhogaḥ śivena mokṣastu viṣṇuneti viniścayaḥ
14 *loke'pi yat prabhurbhuṃkte tanna yacchati karhicit*

अतिप्रियाय तदपि दीयते क्वचिदेव हि ।
नियतार्थ-प्रदानेन तदीयत्वं तदाश्रयः ॥१५॥

atipriyāya tadapi dīyate kvacideva hi
15 *niyatārtha-pradānena tadīyatvaṃ tadāśrayaḥ*

प्रत्येकं साधनञ् चैतद् द्वितीयार्थे महाञ् छ्रमः ।
जीवाः स्वभावतो दुष्टा दोषाभावाय सर्वदा ॥१६॥

pratyekaṃ sādhanañ caitad dvitīyārthe mahāñ chramaḥ
16 *jīvāḥ svabhāvato duṣṭā doṣābhāvāya sarvadā*

They have also been described in their own scriptures
as flawless and replete with all divine virtues.

Even though Shiva and Vishnu
are both able to award enjoyment and liberation, 13
it is quite clear that Shiva grants enjoyment,
while Vishnu bestows liberation.

A powerful person in the world does not give away
that which he cherishes most,
except on rare occasions, and even then 14
he would only give it to someone very dear to him.

Shiva's most treasured asset is liberation,
and so he grants enjoyment.
Vishnu's greatest bliss is his enjoyment with Lakshmi,
and so he awards liberation.

They reward those who belong to them and
who have taken their refuge. 15

There are specific practices
which followers of Shiva and Vishnu
adhere to in order to attain their respective rewards.
It would be troublesome for Shiva or Vishnu
to bestow something that they are not accustomed to giving.

Souls are by their very nature impure.
To become forever free of impurities, 16

श्रवणादि ततः प्रेम्णा सर्वं कार्यं हि सिध्यति ।
मोक्षस्तु सुलभो विष्णोर् भोगश्च शिवतस् तथा ॥१७॥

śravaṇādi tataḥ premṇā sarvaṃ kāryaṃ hi sidhyati
17 *mokṣastu sulabho viṣṇor bhogaśca śivatas tathā*

समर्पणेनाऽत्मनो हि तदीयत्वं भवेद् ध्रुवम् ।
अतदीयतया चाऽपि केवलश्चेत् समाश्रितः ॥१८॥

samarpaṇenā'tmano hi tadīyatvaṃ bhaved dhruvam
18 *atadīyatayā cā'pi kevalaścet samāśritaḥ*

तदाश्रय-तदीयत्व-बुद्ध्यै किञ्चित् समाचरेत् ।
स्वधर्मम् अनुतिष्ठन् वै भारद्वैगुण्यम् अन्यथा ॥१९॥

tadāśraya-tadīyatva-buddhyai kiñcit samācaret
19 *svadharmam anutiṣṭhan vai bhāradvaiguṇyam anyathā*

इत्येवं कथितं सर्वं नैतज्ज्ञाने भ्रमः पुनः ॥२०॥

20 *ityevaṃ kathitaṃ sarvaṃ naitajjñāne bhramaḥ punaḥ*

॥इति श्रीवल्लभाचार्य-विरचितं बालबोधः सम्पूर्णः ॥
iti śrīvallabhācārya-viracitaṃ bālabodhaḥ sampūrṇaḥ

one should practice devotional listening
and other appropriate spiritual practices.
When love arises from all of one's efforts,
everything becomes accomplished.

Know that liberation is easily attained from Vishnu,
and similarly, enjoyment is readily granted by Shiva. 17

Practitioners who dedicate their soul
will certainly attain the exalted position
of belonging to God.
If the divine state of belonging has not arisen,
they should take his shelter
and feel that they belong to him, 18
while observing at least some dharma practices
prescribed for each particular stage of life.
If they fail to attend to these practices,
their burden will be two-fold,
for they will have achieved neither
the spiritual state of belonging
nor the merit of proper action. 19

By understanding all that I have said in this teaching,
confusion concerning the pursuits of life will never arise. 20

Thus ends Bāla Bodhaḥ by Shri Vallabhacharya.

सिद्धान्तमुक्तावली

Siddhānta Muktāvalī

The Pearl Necklace Teachings

Shri Vallabhacharya now moves us directly into the pushti arena with his *Pearl Necklace Teachings*. This doctrine was originally composed around 1498 CE in Jatipura for his disciple Achutyadas, who became the recipient of the highest reward: continual Krishna awareness. In this work, the master reveals the nature of Shri Krishna's seva, the divine act of service to the Beloved. He also gives important empowerments concerning the nature of the world. These teachings are especially useful for bhaktas who want to take an active part in divine service within God's creation but, for their parts to fully unfold, need to understand the subtle relationship between manifest divinity, unmanifested Brahman, and the world.

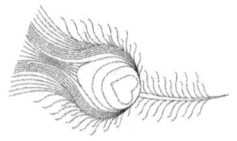

नत्वा हरिं प्रवक्ष्यामि स्वसिद्धान्त-विनिश्चयम् ।
कृष्णसेवा सदा कार्या मानसी सा परा मता ॥१॥

natvā hariṃ pravakṣyāmi svasiddhānta-viniścayam
1 *kṛṣṇasevā sadā kāryā mānasī sā parā matā*

चेतस्तत्प्रवणं सेवा तत्सिद्ध्यै तनु-वित्तजा ।
ततः संसार-दुःखस्य निवृत्तिर् ब्रह्म-बोधनम् ॥२॥

cetastatpravaṇaṃ sevā tatsiddhyai tanu-vittajā
2 *tataḥ saṃsāra-duḥkhasya nivṛttir brahma-bodhanam*

परं ब्रह्म तु कृष्णो हि सच्चिदानन्दकं बृहत् ।
द्विरूपं तद्धि सर्वं स्याद् एकं तस्माद् विलक्षणम् ॥३॥

paraṃ brahma tu kṛṣṇo hi saccidānandakaṃ bṛhat
3 *dvirūpaṃ taddhi sarvaṃ syād ekaṃ tasmād vilakṣaṇam*

अपरं तत्र पूर्वस्मिन् वादिनो बहुधा जगुः ।
मायिकं सगुणं कार्यं स्वतन्त्रं चेति नैकधा ॥४॥

aparaṃ tatra pūrvasmin vādino bahudhā jaguḥ
4 *māyikaṃ saguṇaṃ kāryaṃ svatantraṃ ceti naikadhā*

Having bowed my head to Hari,
I will now tell you my own teachings with great certainty.
Always perform Shri Krishna's pleasing service, or seva.
The highest form of seva is when it
spontaneously fills the mind and heart. 1

This state of being arises
when one's consciousness is threaded into Krishna.
In order to attain this state, bhaktas employ
their bodies and their wealth
in Shri Krishna's beloved service.
Then, the pains of the world are removed,
and knowledge of Brahman arises. 2

Without a doubt, Shri Krishna is supreme Brahman.
The omnipresent Brahman is comprised of
truth, consciousness, and qualified bliss and has two forms.
Brahman is everything in creation
as well as that which is distinct from everything:
the imperishable, formless source. 3

Many contrary opinions about
the nature of this great Brahman have been contrived.
Some argue that this world is an illusion,
while others claim that it is a combination of various attributes.
Some even argue that it is simply an effect,
and others say that the world is independent.
They do not share a common view. 4

तदेवैतत्प्रकारेण भवतीति श्रुतेर्मतम् ।
द्विरूपं चाऽपि गङ्गावज् ज्ञेयं सा जलरूपिणी ॥५॥

tadevaitatprakāreṇa bhavatīti śrutermatam
5 *dvirūpaṃ cā'pi gaṅgāvaj jñeyaṃ sā jalarūpiṇī*

माहात्म्यसंयुता नृणां सेवतां भुक्तिमुक्तिदा ।
मर्यादामार्ग-विधिना तथा ब्रह्मापि बुध्यताम् ॥६॥

māhātmyasaṃyutā nṛṇāṃ sevatāṃ bhuktimuktidā
6 *maryādāmārga-vidhinā tathā brahmāpi budhyatām*

तत्रैव देवता-मूर्तिर् भक्त्या या दृश्यते क्वचित् ।
गङ्गायां च विशेषेण प्रवाहाभेदबुद्धये ॥७॥

tatraiva devatā-mūrtir bhaktyā yā dṛśyate kvacit
7 *gaṅgāyāṃ ca viśeṣeṇa pravāhābhedabuddhaye*

प्रत्यक्षा सा न सर्वेषां प्राकाम्यं स्यात् तया जले ।
विहिताच्च फलात् तद्धि प्रतीत्यापि विशिष्यते ॥८॥

pratyakṣā sā na sarveṣāṃ prākāmyaṃ syāt tayā jale
8 *vihitācca phalāt taddhi pratītyāpi viśiṣyate*

If we look at this world according to the Vedic texts,
we see that it is purely Brahman and has a dual nature
that can be understood from the example of the Ganga River.

One form of the Ganga River is her water. It is seen by all. 5
The second form is that of the holy Ganga,
a place of pilgrimage filled with spiritual greatness.
Practitioners who worship this spiritual form of the Ganga
do so according to the guidelines of the scriptures,
and Ganga grants them enjoyment or even liberation. 6

There is yet a third form of the Ganga River:
her *Devi* (Goddess) aspect.
Her beloved followers
occasionally see her divine form, Ganga Devi,
who is non-separate from her waters,
yet still distinct. 7
The Devi is not seen by all,
but only by her bhaktas.
Through her waters,
which are non-different from her Devi form,
she fulfills their desires.
The experience of coming face to face with the Goddess
is superior to all rewards mentioned in the sacred texts. 8

यथा जलं तथा सर्वं यथा शक्ता तथा बृहत् ।
यथा देवी तथा कृष्णस् तत्राप्येतद् इहोच्यते ॥ ९ ॥

yathā jalaṃ tathā sarvaṃ yathā śaktā tathā bṛhat
9 *yathā devī tathā kṛṣṇas tatrāpyetad ihocyate*

जगत्तु त्रिविधं प्रोक्तं ब्रह्म-विष्णु-शिवास्ततः ।
देवता-रूप-वत् प्रोक्ता ब्रह्मणीत्थं हरिर् मतः ॥ १० ॥

jagattu trividhaṃ proktaṃ brahma-viṣṇu-śivāstataḥ
10 *devatā-rūpa-vat proktā brahmaṇītthaṃ harir mataḥ*

कामचारस्तु लोकेऽस्मिन् ब्रह्मादिभ्यो न चान्यथा ।
परमानन्द-रूपे तु कृष्णे स्वात्मनि निश्चयः ॥ ११ ॥

kāmacārastu loke'smin brahmādibhyo na cānyathā
11 *paramānanda-rūpe tu kṛṣṇe svātmani niścayaḥ*

In this example, understand
the Ganga water to be the visible creation.
The sacred powers
contained within her holy pilgrimage site
are the great Brahman,
while the Goddess Ganga should be understood,
in this analogy, to be the supremely blissful Krishna. 9

As for the nature of the creation,
it has also been spoken of as three-fold,
with Brahma, Vishnu and Shiva as its controlling deities.
The presiding deity of Brahman
is distinct from Brahma, Vishnu, and Shiva,
and is known as Hari—Shri Krishna himself. 10

For attainment of worldly desires, only Brahma the creator
or other bonafide devas should be resorted to.

Without a doubt, one's own inner self is Krishna,
and he is filled with perfect joy. 11

अतस्तु ब्रह्मवादेन कृष्णे बुद्धिर् विधीयताम् ।
आत्मनि ब्रह्मरूपेतु छिद्रा व्योम्नीव चेतनाः ॥१२॥

atastu brahmavādena kṛṣṇe buddhir vidhīyatām
12 *ātmani brahmarūpetu chidrā vyomnīva cetanāḥ*

उपाधिनाशे विज्ञाने ब्रह्मात्मत्वावबोधने ।
गङ्गा-तीर-स्थितो यद्वद् देवतां तत्र पश्यति ॥१३॥

upādhināśe vijñāne brahmātmatvāvabodhane
13 *gaṅgā-tīra-sthito yadvad devatāṃ tatra paśyati*

तथा कृष्णं परं ब्रह्म स्वस्मिन् ज्ञानी प्रपश्यति ।
संसारी यस्तु भजते स दूरस्थो यथा तथा ॥१४॥

tathā kṛṣṇaṃ paraṃ brahma svasmin jñānī prapaśyati
14 *saṃsārī yastu bhajate sa dūrastho yathā tathā*

अपेक्षित-जलादीनाम् अभावात् तत्र दुःखभाक् ।
तस्माच् छ्रीकृष्ण-मार्गस्थो विमुक्तः सर्वलोकतः ॥१५॥

apekṣita-jalādīnām abhāvāt tatra duḥkhabhāk
15 *tasmāc chrīkṛṣṇa-mārgastho vimuktaḥ sarvalokataḥ*

While following the teachings that
everything is Brahman and nothing but Brahman,
blessed ones focus their minds upon Shri Krishna.

Although the self is a pure form of Brahman,
ignorance distorts the individual's cognition of the self,
just as the sky, when viewed through a sieve,
appears to be full of holes. 12
When this limiting ignorance
is eliminated through knowledge,
one awakens to the understanding that
the soul is truly Brahman.

Like someone who stays by the banks of the Ganga
sees the Goddess in the water, 13
similarly, the wise one stands on the banks of the world
and sees Shri Krishna, supreme Brahman,
within the self and the world.

One who worships Ganga
but remains far from her banks
grieves over their distance from her cherished waters. 14
In a similar way, the worldly person
who worships God, yet does not see God
in the world that she lives in, suffers.

The one who treads the blessed path of Shri Krishna's worship
is forever free from the world of bondage. 15

आत्मानन्द-समुद्रस्थं कृष्णमेव विचिन्तयेत् ।
लोकार्थी चेद् भजेत् कृष्णं क्लिष्टो भवति सर्वथा ॥ १६॥

ātmānanda-samudrasthaṃ kṛṣṇameva vicintayet
16 *lokārthī ced bhajet kṛṣṇaṃ kliṣṭo bhavati sarvathā*

क्लिष्टोऽपि चेद् भजेत् कृष्णं लोको नश्यति सर्वथा ।
ज्ञानाऽभावे पुष्टिमार्गी तिष्ठेत् पूजोत्सवादिषु ॥ १७॥

kliṣṭo'pi ced bhajet kṛṣṇaṃ loko naśyati sarvathā
17 *jñānā'bhāve puṣṭimārgī tiṣṭhet pūjotsavādiṣu*

मर्यादास्थस्तु गङ्गायां श्रीभागवत-तत्परः ।
अनुग्रहः पुष्टिमार्गे नियामक इति स्थितिः ॥ १८॥

maryādāsthastu gaṅgāyāṃ śrībhāgavata-tatparaḥ
18 *anugrahaḥ puṣṭimārge niyāmaka iti sthitiḥ*

उभयोस्तु क्रमेणैव पूर्वोक्तैव फलिष्यति ।
ज्ञानाधिको भक्तिमार्ग एवं तस्मात् निरूपितः ॥ १९॥

ubhayostu krameṇaiva pūrvoktaiva phaliṣyati
19 *jñānādhiko bhaktimārga evaṃ tasmāt nirūpitaḥ*

He blissfully contemplates Shri Krishna,
who lives in the ocean of his own joy.

Those who worship Shri Krishna for worldly reasons
always encounter difficulties, 16
while those who worship Shri Krishna amidst difficulties
have every worldly obstruction obliterated.

If a follower of the path of grace is devoid of knowledge,
then they should remain in a place
where pujas and celebrations are performed. 17

The follower of the lawful path, on the other hand,
should enhance their practice by staying near the Ganga River
and reviewing the teachings of the devotional text,
Shrimad Bhagavatam. In every situation,
know that grace rules the blessed path. 18

Both of these types of practitioners
can attain the supreme reward.
It is clearly explained, however, that
the path of loving devotion (*bhakti*)
is superior to the path of knowledge (*jñāna*). 19

भक्त्यभावे तु तीरस्थो यथा दुष्टैः स्वकर्मभिः ।
अन्यथाभावमापन्नस् तस्मात् स्थानाच्च नश्यति ॥२०॥

bhaktyabhāve tu tīrastho yathā duṣṭaiḥ svakarmabhiḥ
20 *anyathābhāvamāpannas tasmāt sthānācca naśyati*

एवं स्वशास्त्र-सर्वस्वं मया गुप्तं निरूपितम् ।
एतद् बुद्ध्वा विमुच्येत पुरुषः सर्व-संशयात् ॥२१॥

evaṃ svaśāstra-sarvasvaṃ mayā guptaṃ nirūpitam
21 *etad buddhvā vimucyeta puruṣaḥ sarva-saṃśayāt*

॥इति श्रीवल्लभाचार्य-विरचिता सिद्धान्तमुक्तावली सम्पूर्णा ॥
iti śrīvallabhācārya-viracitā siddhāntamuktāvalī sampūrṇā

Just as a devotionally ignorant person
who performs evil deeds by the Ganga
destroys himself as well as the sanctity of the place,
one who lives in this sacred world without devotion
does not attain any spiritual goals
and descends into darkness. 20

In this way I have revealed
my all-encompassing secret doctrine.
By understanding it, one becomes free of any doubt. 21

Thus ends Siddhānta Muktāvalī by Shri Vallabhacharya.

पुष्टिप्रवाहमर्यादा

Puṣṭi Pravāha Maryādā

The Paths of Grace, Mundane Flow, and Lawful Limitations

Now Shri Vallabhacharya brings us further into his grace filled world by describing the different natures of beings. At the absolute level, everything is Brahman, but souls appear in this world with various temperaments. Their paths and rewards are all unique. By recognizing the variety of souls, their origins and activities, we can further understand and then develop our own devotion. In the master's words:

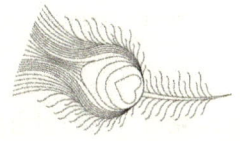

पुष्टि-प्रवाह-मर्यादा विशेषेण पृथक् पृथक् ॥
जीव-देह-क्रिया-भेदैः प्रवाहेण फलेन च ॥१॥

puṣṭi-pravāha-maryādā viśeṣeṇa pṛthak pṛthak
1 *jīva-deha-kriyā-bhedaiḥ pravāheṇa phalena ca*

वक्ष्यामि सर्वसन्देहा न भविष्यन्ति यच्छ्रुतेः ।
भक्तिमार्गस्य कथनात् पुष्टिरस्तीति निश्चयः ॥२॥

vakṣyāmi sarvasandehā na bhaviṣyanti yacchruteḥ
2 *bhaktimārgasya kathanāt puṣṭirastīti niścayaḥ*

द्वौ भूतसर्गा-वित्युक्तेः प्रवाहोऽपि व्यवस्थितः ।
वेदस्य विद्यमानत्वान् मर्यादापि व्यवस्थिता ॥३॥

dvau bhūtasargā-vityukteḥ pravāho'pi vyavasthitaḥ
3 *vedasya vidyamānatvān maryādāpi vyavasthitā*

कश्चिदेव हि भक्तो हि यो मद्भक्त इतीरणात् ।
सर्वत्रोत्कर्ष-कथनात् पुष्टिरस्तीति निश्चयः ॥४॥

kaścideva hi bhakto hi yo madbhakta itīraṇāt
4 *sarvatrotkarṣa-kathanāt puṣṭirastīti niścayaḥ*

Those who belong to the paths of grace (*puṣṭi*),
mundane flow (*pravāha*), and lawful limitations (*maryādā*)
each have distinct souls, bodies, actions,
movements, and rewards. 1
I will now explain their differences,
and those who hear my teachings
will have all uncertainties removed.

The path of devotion has been mentioned in the scriptures,
and from those passages we know without a doubt
that the grace of God exists. 2

In the *Bhagavad Gita*, Lord Krishna tells Arjuna,
"In this world, there are two types of souls: godly and ungodly."
From this statement, we can affirm the existence of
ungodly souls who follow the path of worldly flow.

The presence of the Vedas establishes the existence of
the path of lawful limitations. 3

Shri Krishna says in the *Bhagavad Gita*,
"My bhakta is very dear to me."
Only certain souls are true bhaktas.
Everywhere there are mentions of bhakti being exalted,
and this proves without a doubt the existence of grace. 4

न सर्वोऽतः प्रवाहाद्धि भिन्नो वेदाच्च भेदतः ।
यदा यस्येति वचनान् नाहं वेदैर् इतीरणात् ॥५॥

na sarvo'taḥ pravāhāddhi bhinno vedācca bhedataḥ
5 *yadā yasyeti vacanān nāhaṃ vedair itīraṇāt*

मार्गैकत्वेऽपि चेदन्त्यौ तनू भक्त्यागमौ मतौ ।
न तद् युक्तं सूत्रतोहि भिन्नो युक्त्या हि वैदिकः ॥६॥

mārgaikatve'pi cedantyau tanū bhaktyāgamau matau
6 *na tad yuktaṃ sūtratohi bhinno yuktyā hi vaidikaḥ*

जीवदेहकृतीनां च भिन्नत्वं नित्यताश्रुतेः ।
यथा तद्वत् पुष्टिमार्गे द्वयोरपि निषेधतः ॥७॥

jīvadehakṛtīnāṃ ca bhinnatvaṃ nityatāśruteḥ
7 *yathā tadvat puṣṭimārge dvayorapi niṣedhataḥ*

प्रमाणभेदाद् भिन्नो हि पुष्टिमार्गो निरूपितः ।
सर्गभेदं प्रवक्ष्यामि स्वरूपाऽङ्ग-क्रियायुतम् ॥८॥

pramāṇabhedād bhinno hi puṣṭimārgo nirūpitaḥ
8 *sargabhedaṃ pravakṣyāmi svarūpā'ṅga-kriyāyutam*

इच्छामात्रेण मनसा प्रवाहं सृष्टवान् हरिः ।
वचसा वेदमार्गं हि पुष्टिं कायेन निश्चयः ॥९॥

icchāmātreṇa manasā pravāhaṃ sṛṣṭavān hariḥ
9 *vacasā vedamārgaṃ hi puṣṭiṃ kāyena niścayaḥ*

Grace filled souls are distinct from souls in the worldly flow
as well as from law abiding Vedic practitioners.
The *Shrimad Bhagavatam* confirms this with the statement,
"When the Lord graces someone, that individual
abandons the ways of the world and Vedas."
Shri Krishna also tells Arjuna, "This divine form of mine
cannot be seen by knowing the Vedas." 5

The *Sutras* (sacred texts) have clearly explained
the particularities of these three paths.
Sacred Vedic texts do not support the views of those
who believe that the three paths are really one
and are all a part of devotion. 6

According to the *Shrutis* (sacred texts),
the souls, bodies, and actions
of the three different types of souls are forever different.
From these proofs, it is established that
the path of grace is separate from the other two paths. 7

Other valid scriptural passages also narrate
the distinct nature of the path of grace.

Now hear the differences in origin
of the souls, bodies, and actions
of these different types of beings. 8

The blessed Lord created the path of worldly flow
with his mere wish, with his mind (*manas*).
With his speech (*vacas*) he created
the path of lawful limitations, and without a doubt,
the path of grace came forth from his bliss form (*kāya*). 9

मूलेच्छातः फलं लोके वेदोक्तं वैदिकेऽपि च ।
कायेन तु फलं पुष्टौ भिन्नेच्छातोऽपि नैकता ॥ १० ॥

mūlecchātaḥ phalaṃ loke vedoktaṃ vaidike'pi ca
10 *kāyena tu phalaṃ puṣṭau bhinnecchāto'pi naikatā*

तानहं द्विषतो वाक्याद् भिन्ना जीवाः प्रवाहिणः ।
अत एवेतरौ भिन्नौ सान्तौ मोक्षप्रवेशतः ॥ ११ ॥

tānahaṃ dviṣato vākyād bhinnā jīvāḥ pravāhiṇaḥ
11 *ata evetarau bhinnau sāntau mokṣapraveśataḥ*

तस्माज् जीवाः पूष्टिमार्गे भिन्नाएव न संशयः ।
भगवद्-रूप-सेवार्थं तत्-सृष्टिर् नान्यथा भवेत् ॥ १२ ॥

tasmāj jīvāḥ pūṣṭimārge bhinnāeva na saṃśayaḥ
12 *bhagavad-rūpa-sevārthaṃ tat-sṛṣṭir nānyathā bhavet*

स्वरूपेणावतारेण लिङ्गेन च गुणेन च ।
तारतम्यं न स्वरूपे देहे वा तत्क्रियासु वा ॥ १३ ॥

svarūpeṇāvatāreṇa liṅgena ca guṇena ca
13 *tāratamyaṃ na svarūpe dehe vā tatkriyāsu vā*

Worldly based desires bear worldly rewards.
Lawful rewards are described in the Vedas, while
the grace filled fruit arises from the Lord's own bliss form.
Due to the different desires of each path,
the rewards which arise are never the same. 10

Shri Krishna says in the *Gita*,
"I repeatedly cast those ungodly,
cruel hearted souls into demonical wombs."
This passage demonstrates that worldly souls are different
from the souls who follow the paths of law or grace,
who ultimately can attain freedom from rebirth. 11

Therefore, souls on the path of grace
are undoubtedly different from the other two types.
The creation of grace filled souls is strictly
for the loving service of the blessed, blissful Lord. 12

There is no remarkable difference between the Lord's form,
his incarnation, the markings on his body, his virtues,
and the bhaktas' souls, bodies and actions. 13

तथापि यावता कार्यं तावत् तस्य करोति हि।
ते हि द्विधा शुद्ध-मिश्र-भेदान् मिश्रास् त्रिधा पुनः॥१४॥

tathāpi yāvatā kāryaṃ tāvat tasya karoti hi
14 *te hi dvidhā śuddha-miśra-bhedān miśrās tridhā punaḥ*

प्रवाहादि-विभेदेन भगवत्कार्य-सिद्धये।
पुष्ट्या विमिश्राः सर्वज्ञाः प्रवाहेण क्रियारताः॥१५॥

pravāhādi-vibhedena bhagavatkārya-siddhaye
15 *puṣṭyā vimiśrāḥ sarvajñāḥ pravāheṇa kriyāratāḥ*

मर्यादया गुणज्ञास्ते शुद्धाः प्रेम्णातिदुर्लुभाः।
एवं सर्गस्तु तेषां हि फलं त्वत्र निरूप्यते॥१६॥

maryādayā guṇajñāste śuddhāḥ premṇātidurlubhāḥ
16 *evaṃ sargastu teṣāṃ hi phalaṃ tvatra nirūpyate*

भगवानेव हि फलं स यथाविर्भवेद् भुवि।
गुणस्वरूपभेदेन तथा तेषां फलं भवेत्॥१७॥

bhagavāneva hi phalaṃ sa yathāvirbhaved bhuvi
17 *guṇasvarūpabhedena tathā teṣāṃ phalaṃ bhavet*

आसक्तौ भगवानेव शापं दापयति क्वचित्।
अहङ्कारेऽथवा लोके तन्मार्ग-स्थापनाय हि॥१८॥

āsaktau bhagavāneva śāpaṃ dāpayati kvacit
18 *ahaṅkāre'thavā loke tanmārga-sthāpanāya hi*

Still, the blessed one creates souls
according to the types of activities they will undertake.
The grace filled creation is two-fold: either mixed or pure.

The 'mixed' grace filled souls fall into three categories. 14
The blessed one created divine, worldly, and lawful souls
to fulfill his own purpose.

Those souls who are grace combined with grace
are all-knowing.
Those who are souls of grace mixed with worldly flow
are inclined towards action. 15

The souls of grace who are mixed with law
are knowers of God's attributes.

The one who becomes pure pushti
through love alone is very rare.
In this way, understand how the grace filled ones arise.
Now hear about their rewards. 16

Shri Krishna himself is their reward.
He appears before them here on earth,
with various forms and attributes,
in order to give them their particular rewards. 17

Sometimes the blessed Lord may
put a curse on a blessed follower
who has become prideful or falsely attached,
in order to reestablish him or her back
upon the path in this world. 18

न ते पाषण्डतां यान्ति न च रोगाद्युपद्रवः ।
महानुभावाः प्रायेण शास्त्रं शुद्धत्व-हेतवे ॥१९॥

na te pāṣaṇḍatāṃ yānti na ca rogādyupadravaḥ
19 *mahānubhāvāḥ prāyeṇa śāstraṃ śuddhatva-hetave*

भगवत् तारतम्येन तारतम्यं भजन्ति हि ।
लौकिकत्वं वैदिकत्वं कापट्यात् तेषु नान्यथा ॥२०॥

bhagavat tāratamyena tāratamyaṃ bhajanti hi
20 *laukikatvaṃ vaidikatvaṃ kāpaṭyāt teṣu nānyathā*

वैष्णवत्वं हि सहजं ततोऽन्यत्र विपर्ययः ।
सम्बन्धिनस्तु ये जीवाः प्रवाहस्थास् तथाऽपरे ॥२१॥

vaiṣṇavatvaṃ hi sahajaṃ tato'nyatra viparyayaḥ
21 *sambandhinastu ye jīvāḥ pravāhasthās tathā'pare*

चर्षणी शब्द वाच्यास्ते ते सर्वे सर्ववर्त्मसु ।
क्षणात् सर्वत्वमायान्ति रुचिस् तेषां न कुत्रचित् ॥२२॥

carṣaṇī śabda vācyāste te sarve sarvavartmasu
22 *kṣaṇāt sarvatvamāyānti rucis teṣāṃ na kutracit*

तेषां क्रियानुसारेण सर्वत्र सकलं फलम् ।
प्रवाहस्थान् प्रवक्ष्यामि स्वरूपाङ्ग-क्रियायुतान् ॥२३॥

teṣāṃ kriyānusāreṇa sarvatra sakalaṃ phalam
23 *pravāhasthān pravakṣyāmi svarūpāṅga-kriyāyutān*

Grace filled souls do not act in a contrary way,
nor do they experience disease or complications.
They generally become beings with profound experience,
and God's teachings are given to them for purification. 19

Bhaktas worship the blessed Lord
according to the way he manifests.
The worldly and Vedic activities they perform
are nothing but an outward show,
devoid of true heart connection. 20

For them, the loving path of devotion,
the Vaishnava dharma, is perfectly natural,
and everything else seems incompatible.

There is yet another type of soul who,
although being established in worldly flow,
flirts with all of the paths. 21
I call them wanderers.
They jump from one path to another,
staying on each one for but a moment.
They do not savor or feel attachment anywhere. 22
According to their scattered actions,
they always receive partial rewards.

Now I will describe the worldly soul's
inner being, body, and actions. 23

जीवास्ते ह्यासुराः सर्वे प्रवृत्तिं चेति वर्णिताः ।
ते च द्विधा प्रकीर्त्यन्ते ह्यज्ञ-दुर्ज्ञ-विभेदतः ॥२४॥

jīvāste hyāsurāḥ sarve pravṛttiṃ ceti varṇitāḥ
24 *te ca dvidhā prakīrtyante hyajña-durjña-vibhedataḥ*

दुर्ज्ञास्ते भगवत्प्रोक्ता ह्यज्ञास्तान्-अनु ये पुनः ।
प्रवाहेऽपि समागत्य पुष्टिस्थस् तैर् न युज्यते ॥२५॥

durjñāste bhagavatproktā hyajñāstān-anu ye punaḥ
25 *pravāhe'pi samāgatya puṣṭisthas tair na yujyate*

सोऽपि तैस्-तत्कुले जातः कर्मणा जायते यतः ।

26a *so'pi tais-tatkule jātaḥ karmaṇā jāyate yataḥ*

॥इति श्रीवल्लभाचार्य-विरचिता पुष्टिप्रवाहमर्यादा सम्पूर्णा ॥
iti śrīvallabhācārya-viracitā puṣṭipravāhamaryādā sampūrṇā

Krishna speaks of them in the *Gita*:
"They do not know what to do or what not to do.
They are devoid of purity, good conduct, and truth."

These ungodly souls are of two types:
the ignorant and the truly wicked. 24

Shri Krishna has already described in the *Gita*
the nature of the purely wicked.

Those who are merely ignorant
emulate the ways of the wicked
but are not really demonical.

A divine soul who is born into a family full of worldly beings
does not remain on the family's path, but on the path of grace. 25
That soul's previous karmas were responsible
for their birth, but not for their spiritual path. 26a

Thus ends Puṣṭi Pravāha Maryādā by Shri Vallabhacharya.[*]

---

* Translator's note: This treatise by Shri Vallabhacharya is incomplete.

सिद्धान्तरहस्यम्

Siddhānta Rahasyam

The Secret Doctrine

Shrimad Vallabhacharya's *Secret Doctrine* is Shri Krishna's direct response to the master's concern about how divine souls can achieve their blissful Lord during this impure age of struggle known as the Kali Yuga. Shri Krishna himself established the foundations of the path of grace on this auspicious night in 1492 CE, when he appeared before Shri Vallabhacharya by the banks of the Yamuna River in the sacred town of Gokul. The secrets of soulful dedication and divine connection are revealed in the following eight verses.

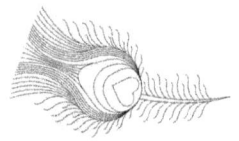

श्रावणस्याऽमले पक्षे एकादश्यां महानिशि ।
साक्षाद् भगवता प्रोक्तं तदक्षरश उच्यते ॥ १॥

śrāvaṇasyā'male pakṣe ekādaśyāṃ mahāniśi
1 *sākṣād bhagavatā proktaṃ tadakṣaraśa ucyate*

ब्रह्मसम्बन्ध-करणात् सर्वेषां देहजीवयोः ।
सर्वदोष-निवृत्तिर् हि दोषाः पञ्चविधाः स्मृताः ॥ २॥

brahmasambandha-karaṇāt sarveṣāṃ dehajīvayoḥ
2 *sarvadoṣa-nivṛttir hi doṣāḥ pañcavidhāḥ smṛtāḥ*

सहजा देश-कालोत्थाः लोक-वेद-निरूपिताः ।
संयोगजाः स्पर्शजाश्च न मन्तव्याः कथञ्चन ॥ ३॥

sahajā deśa-kālotthāḥ loka-veda-nirūpitāḥ
3 *saṃyogajāḥ sparśajāśca na mantavyāḥ kathañcana*

अन्यथा सर्वदोषाणां न निवृत्तिः कथञ्चन ।
असमर्पित-वस्तूनां तस्माद् वर्जनम् आचरेत् ॥ ४॥

anyathā sarvadoṣāṇāṃ na nivṛttiḥ kathañcana
4 *asamarpita-vastūnāṃ tasmād varjanam ācaret*

निवेदिभिः समर्प्यैव सर्वं कुर्याद् इति स्थितिः ।
न मतं देवदेवस्य सामिभुक्त-समर्पणम् ॥ ५॥

nivedibhiḥ samarpyaiva sarvaṃ kuryād iti sthitiḥ
5 *na mataṃ devadevasya sāmibhukta-samarpaṇam*

At midnight on the eleventh lunar day,
during the bright half of the month of Shravan,
Shri Krishna appeared before me.
I will now reveal the words he spoke. 1

Shri Krishna explained to me that
after taking Brahma Sambandha initiation
and thereby establishing a connection to Brahman,
the impurities of the soul are completely removed.
These impurities are said to be of five kinds. 2

As explained in Vedic and worldly texts,
these five impurities are natural impurities
as well as those related to
time, place, association, and physical contact.
After taking Brahma Sambandha,
they should no longer be considered valid. 3

These impurities can never be removed
without connection to Brahman.
Therefore, anything that has not been offered to God
should not be used. 4

Dedicated souls should perform all activities
by first offering them to the blessed Lord.
This is the way a bhakta should always live.

Anything that has been previously enjoyed
should never be offered to Shri Krishna,
the supreme Lord of all the devas. 5

तस्माद् आदौ सर्वकार्ये सर्ववस्तु-समर्पणम् ।
दत्तापहार-वचनं तथा च सकलं हरेः ॥६॥

tasmād ādau sarvakārye sarvavastu-samarpaṇam
6 *dattāpahāra-vacanaṃ tathā ca sakalaṃ hareḥ*

न ग्राह्यमिति वाक्यं हि भिन्नमार्गपरं मतम् ।
सेवकानां यथा लोके व्यवहारः प्रसिध्यति ॥७॥

na grāhyamiti vākyaṃ hi bhinnamārgaparaṃ matam
7 *sevakānāṃ yathā loke vyavahāraḥ prasidhyati*

तथा कार्यं समर्प्यैव सर्वेषां ब्रह्मता ततः ।
गङ्गात्वं सर्वदोषाणां गुणदोषादि-वर्णना ॥८॥

tathā kāryaṃ samarpyaiva sarveṣāṃ brahmatā tataḥ
8 *gaṅgātvaṃ sarvadoṣāṇāṃ guṇadoṣādi-varṇanā*

गङ्गात्वेन निरुप्या स्यात् तद् वद् अत्रापि चैव हि ॥९॥

9 *gaṅgātvena nirupyā syāt tad vad atrāpi caiva hi*

॥इति श्रीवल्लभाचार्य-विरचितं श्रीसिद्धान्तरहस्यं सम्पूर्णम् ॥
iti śrīvallabhācārya-viracitaṃ śrīsiddhāntarahasyaṃ sampūrṇam

Therefore, at the start of any undertaking,
everything should first be dedicated to him.
The statement that says,
"It is all his and therefore cannot be used," 6
holds no validity here and refers to another path.

Just like good servants in the world
are known for their selfless service, 7
the bhakta selflessly offers herself in every undertaking,
and then everything becomes godly for her.

Like impure water that joins with the Ganga
becomes sacred Ganga
and is no longer considered pure or impure, 8
similarly, everything that is offered to God
becomes God: perfectly divine. 9

Thus ends Siddhānta Rahasyam by Shri Vallabhacharya.

नवरत्नम्

Navaratnam

Nine Jewels

Shri Vallabhacharya composed *Nine Jewels* around 1501 CE in Adel for his disciple Govinda Dube, in order to remove the anxieties that were obstructing his blessed worship. Shri Vallabhacharya's advice is clear: when you have dedicated yourself to Shri Krishna, there is simply nothing to worry about. Anxiety always obstructs the flow of devotion. The recitation of this text puts the bhakta's mind and heart at ease.

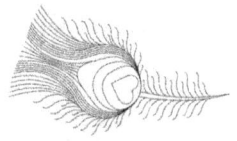

चिन्ता काऽपि न कार्या निवेदितात्मभिः कदापीति ।
भगवानपि पुष्टिस्थो न करिष्यति लौकिकीं च गतिम् ॥ १॥

cintā kā'pi na kāryā niveditātmabhiḥ kadāpīti
1 *bhagavānapi puṣṭistho na kariṣyati laukikīṃ ca gatim*

निवेदनं तु स्मर्तव्यं सर्वथा तादृशैर्जनैः ।
सर्वेश्वरश्च सर्वात्मा निजेच्छातः करिष्यति ॥ २॥

nivedanaṃ tu smartavyaṃ sarvathā tādṛśairjanaiḥ
2 *sarveśvaraśca sarvātmā nijecchātaḥ kariṣyati*

सर्वेषां प्रभुसम्बन्धो न प्रत्येकमिति स्थितिः ।
अतोऽन्य विनियोगेऽपि चिन्ता का स्वस्य सोऽपि चेत् ॥ ३॥

sarveṣāṃ prabhusambandho na pratyekamiti sthitiḥ
3 *ato'nya viniyoge'pi cintā kā svasya so'pi cet*

अज्ञानाद् अथवा ज्ञानात् कृतम् आत्मनिवेदनम् ।
यैः कृष्णसात्कृत प्राणैस् तेषां का परिदेवना ॥ ४॥

ajñānād athavā jñānāt kṛtam ātmanivedanam
4 *yaiḥ kṛṣṇasātkṛta prāṇais teṣāṃ kā paridevanā*

तथा निवेदने चिन्ता त्याज्या श्रीपुरुषोत्तमे ।
विनियोगेऽपि सा त्याज्या समर्थो हि हरिः स्वतः ॥ ५॥

tathā nivedane cintā tyājyā śrīpuruṣottame
5 *viniyoge'pi sā tyājyā samartho hi hariḥ svataḥ*

Those who have dedicated their very selves
should never worry,
because the blessed Lord,
who is established in grace,
will never give them a mundane life. 1

Remember your dedication
in the company of other accomplished bhaktas.
The supreme being, Shri Krishna, the self of all,
will do as he pleases and
will fulfill his bhaktas' desires. 2

Everything is connected to God,
and nothing can ever remain separate from him.
And so if you engage in activities or connections
that don't seem related to him,
there is no reason to worry,
because actually, they are. 3

If those who have dedicated themselves
with or without proper understanding
should have no concerns,
then what to say of those who have established
their very life force (*prāṇa*) with Krishna? 4

Concerns regarding one's dedication, as well as
anxieties regarding any other involvements in life,
should be given over to Shri Krishna.
These worries should be renounced, because
Hari himself is totally capable
of taking care of his own bhaktas. 5

लोके स्वास्थ्यं तथा वेदे हरिस्तु न करिष्यति ।
पुष्टिमार्गस्थितो यस्मात् साक्षिणो भवताऽखिलाः ॥ ६॥

loke svāsthyaṃ tathā vede haristu na kariṣyati
6 *puṣṭimārgasthito yasmāt sākṣiṇo bhavatā'khilāḥ*

सेवाकृतिर् गुरोर् आज्ञा बाधनं वा हरीच्छया ।
अतः सेवापरं चित्तं विधाय स्थीयतां सुखम् ॥ ७॥

sevākṛtir guror ājñā bādhanaṃ vā harīcchayā
7 *ataḥ sevāparaṃ cittaṃ vidhāya sthīyatāṃ sukham*

चित्तोद्वेगं विधायाऽपि हरिर् यद्यत् करिष्यति ।
तथैव तस्य लीलेति मत्वा चिंतां द्रुतं त्यजेत् ॥ ८॥

cittodvegaṃ vidhāyā'pi harir yadyat kariṣyati
8 *tathaiva tasya līleti matvā cintāṃ drutaṃ tyajet*

तस्मात् सर्वात्मना नित्यं श्रीकृष्णः शरणं मम ।
वदद्भिर् एवं सततं स्थेयम् इत्येव मे मतिः ॥ ९॥

tasmāt sarvātmanā nityaṃ śrīkṛṣṇaḥ śaraṇaṃ mama
9 *vadadbhir evaṃ satataṃ stheyam ityeva me matiḥ*

॥इति श्रीवल्लभाचार्य-विरचितं नवरत्नं सम्पूर्णम् ॥
iti śrīvallabhācārya-viracitaṃ navaratnaṃ sampūrṇam

Shri Krishna, who is established in grace,
will not allow his bhaktas
to feel at peace with themselves
in the mundane world or in the path of the Vedas.
Therefore, all grace filled beings
should remain a mere witness (*sākṣi*)
to whatever happens. 6

Perform seva according to the guru's instructions.
If for some reason seva cannot be performed
as per the guru's directions,
consider this to be the wish of Hari.
One should, however, keep one's mind
absorbed in seva and remain happy. 7

If for some reason
Hari creates a situation that makes you anxious,
understand that he does everything
according to his own lila.
Know that everything arises
according to his lila plan and
relinquish anxiety immediately. 8

Therefore, with total love,
feel Shri Krishna everywhere
and continually recite, "Shri Krishna is my refuge."
This is my firm conviction. 9

Thus ends Navaratnam by Shri Vallabhacharya.

अन्तःकरणप्रबोधः

Antaḥkaraṇa Prabodhaḥ

An Appeal to My Heart

In this text, Shri Vallabhacharya consoles his own heart. Shri Krishna has requested him to leave this world and return to him, but the bhakti master decides to delay his divine return, in order to fulfill his devotional mission on earth to complete *Shri Subodhiniji*, his commentary on Shri Krishna's lilas as depicted in the *Shrimad Bhagavatam*. In this appeal to his own heart, the master brilliantly reflects on his relationship with Lord Krishna.

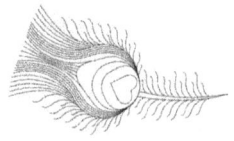

अन्तःकरण मद्वाक्यं सावधानतया शृणु ।
कृष्णात् परं नास्ति दैवं वस्तुतो दोषवर्जितम् ॥ १॥

antaḥkaraṇa madvākyaṃ sāvadhānatayā śṛṇu
1 *kṛṣṇāt paraṃ nāsti daivaṃ vastuto doṣavarjitam*

चाण्डाली चेद् राजपत्नी जाता राज्ञा च मानिता ।
कदाचिदपमानेऽपि मूलतः का क्षतिर्भवेत् ॥ २॥

cāṇḍālī ced rājapatnī jātā rājñā ca mānitā
2 *kadācidapamāne'pi mūlataḥ kā kṣatirbhavet*

समर्पणाद् अहं पूर्वम् उत्तमः किं सदा स्थितः ।
का ममाधमता भाव्या पश्चात्तापो यतो भवेत् ॥ ३॥

samarpaṇād ahaṃ pūrvam uttamaḥ kiṃ sadā sthitaḥ
3 *kā mamādhamatā bhāvyā paścāttāpo yato bhavet*

O heart, listen carefully to my words!
Besides Shri Krishna,
there is no flawless deva. 1

If an outcaste woman
were to become a queen
and be honored by her king,
but then at some point
her king becomes displeased with her,
she is still far better off
than when she was an outcaste. 2

Was I always exalted
before I dedicated myself to you?
Now, after my dedication,
have I become so fallen
that I should repent?
Of course not! 3

सत्यसङ्कल्पतो विष्णुर् नान्यथा तु करिष्यति ।
आज्ञैव कार्या सततं स्वामिद्रोहोऽन्यथा भवेत् ॥४॥

satyasaṅkalpato viṣṇur nānyathā tu kariṣyati
4 *ājñaiva kāryā satataṃ svāmidroho'nyathā bhavet*

सेवकस्य तु धर्मोऽयं स्वामी स्वस्य करिष्यति ।
आज्ञा पूर्वं तु या जाता गङ्गा-सागर-सङ्गमे ॥५॥

sevakasya tu dharmo'yaṃ svāmī svasya kariṣyati
5 *ājñā pūrvaṃ tu yā jātā gaṅgā-sāgara-saṅgame*

याऽपि पश्चान् मधुवने न कृतं तद् द्वयं मया ।
देह-देश-परित्यागस् तृतीयो लोकगोचरः ॥६॥

yā'pi paścān madhuvane na kṛtaṃ tad dvayaṃ mayā
6 *deha-deśa-parityāgas tṛtīyo lokagocaraḥ*

पश्चात्तापः कथं तत्र सेवकोऽहं न चान्यथा ।
लौकिकप्रभुवत्-कृष्णो न द्रष्टव्यः कदाचन ॥७॥

paścāttāpaḥ kathaṃ tatra sevako'haṃ na cānyathā
7 *laukikaprabhuvat-kṛṣṇo na draṣṭavyaḥ kadācana*

I know that whatever the blessed Lord promises
always comes to be.
He never acts contrary to his promise.
His command should always be followed.
Otherwise, one becomes guilty of
transgressing the master of all things. 4
This is the duty of the follower.
Know that the blessed Lord himself
will accomplish whatever else needs to be done.

I did not follow my Lord's command
to leave my body at Ganga Sagar,
where the river meets the sea. 5

Nor did I obey his second command
at Madhuvan, near Mathura,
to leave that place and return to him.
Upon his third request
for me to renounce this visible world,
I will surely oblige. 6

Why should I lament now?
I am his follower and nothing else.

Shri Krishna should never be viewed
as a worldly being. 7

सर्वं समर्पितं भक्त्या कृतार्थोऽसि सुखी भव।
प्रौढापि दुहिता यद्वत् स्नेहान् न प्रेष्यते वरे॥८॥

sarvaṃ samarpitaṃ bhaktyā kṛtārtho'si sukhī bhava
8 *prauḍhāpi duhitā yadvat snehān na preṣyate vare*

तथा देहे न कर्तव्यं वरस् तुष्यति नान्यथा।
लोकवच्चेत् स्थितिर् मे स्यात् किं स्याद् इति विचारय॥९॥

tathā dehe na kartavyaṃ varas-tuṣyati nānyathā
9 *lokavaccet sthitir me syāt kiṃ syād iti vicāraya*

अशक्ये हरिरेवाऽस्ति मोहं मा गाः कथञ्चन॥१०॥

10 *aśakye harirevā'sti mohaṃ mā gāḥ kathañcana*

इति श्रीकृष्णदासस्य वल्लभस्य हितं वचः।
चित्तं प्रति यदाकर्ण्य भक्तो निश्चिन्ततां व्रजेत्॥११॥

iti śrīkṛṣṇadāsasya vallabhasya hitaṃ vacaḥ
11 *cittaṃ prati yadākarṇya bhakto niścintatāṃ vrajet*

॥इति श्रीवल्लभाचार्य-विरचितो अन्तःकरणप्रबोधः सम्पूर्णः॥
iti śrīvallabhācārya-viracito antaḥkaraṇaprabodhaḥ sampūrṇaḥ

O heart, you have already
dedicated everything to him with devotion.
You have accomplished your goal, so be content.

If a father does not send his married daughter
to be with her husband
out of excessive affection for her,
her husband will be displeased. 8
Similarly, my husband, Shri Krishna,
will not be pleased with me
if I do not follow my bodily duty
and return to him.
I should consider my divine situation
in terms of the ways of the world:
a bride should go to her husband and nowhere else.
If I do not act accordingly with Shri Krishna,
tell me, where will I stand? 9

Let there be no confusion here.
In the impossible, Hari alone is capable. 10

In this way, I, Shri Krishna's beloved follower,
have given my heart some good guidance.
If bhaktas listen to these words,
they will become free of any concern. 11

Thus ends Antaḥkaraṇa Prabodhaḥ by Shri Vallabhacharya.

विवेकधैर्याश्रयः

Viveka Dhairyāśrayaḥ

Wisdom, Perseverance, and Refuge

Wisdom, perseverance, and refuge are the three main devotional ingredients that create and maintain the firm mood of devotion. In this teaching, Shri Vallabhacharya gives us a practical guide filled with wise advice on how to live in the world, deal with obstructions, and maintain a rich devotional life. In a discrete way, this work also addresses the higher devotional states which flourish between the Beloved and his loved ones.

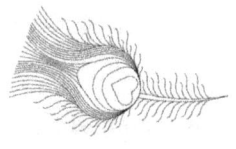

विवेक-धैर्ये सततं रक्षणीये तथाश्रयः।
विवेकस्तु हरिः सर्वं निजेच्छातः करिष्यति ॥१॥

viveka-dhairye satataṃ rakṣaṇīye tathāśrayaḥ
1 *vivekastu hariḥ sarvaṃ nijecchātaḥ kariṣyati*

प्रार्थिते वा ततः किं स्यात् स्वाम्यभिप्राय-संशयात्।
सर्वत्र तस्य सर्वं हि सर्वसामर्थ्यमेव च ॥२॥

prārthite vā tataḥ kiṃ syāt svāmyabhiprāya-saṃśayāt
2 *sarvatra tasya sarvaṃ hi sarvasāmarthyameva ca*

अभिमानश्च संत्याज्यः स्वाम्यधीनत्व-भावनात्।
विशेषतश्चेद् आज्ञा स्याद् अन्तःकरणगोचरः ॥३॥

abhimānaśca santyājyaḥ svāmyadhīnatva-bhāvanāt
3 *viśeṣataśced ājñā syād antaḥkaraṇagocaraḥ*

तदा विशेषगत्यादि भाव्यं भिन्नं तु दैहिकात्।
आपद्-गत्यादि-कार्येषु हठस् त्याज्यश्च सर्वथा ॥४॥

tadā viśeṣagatyādi bhāvyaṃ bhinnaṃ tu daihikāt
4 *āpad-gatyādi-kāryeṣu haṭhas tyājyaśca sarvathā*

अनाग्रहश्च सर्वत्र धर्माधर्माऽग्र-दर्शनम्।
विवेकोऽयं समाख्यातो धैर्यं तु विनिरूप्यते ॥५॥

anāgrahaśca sarvatra dharmādharmā'gra-darśanam
5 *viveko'yaṃ samākhyāto dhairyaṃ tu vinirūpyate*

Always protect your discrimination and perseverance,
and carefully nourish divine refuge.
True wisdom is seeing that beloved Hari
will accomplish everything according to his own will. 1

What is the use of prayer?
Why request something from him?
This only happens when there is a doubt
in the intention of his perfect plan.
Hari is everywhere, and he is everything.
He is compelling and potent. 2

Leave completely all sense of false pride
and cherish the feeling of being under Hari's rule.
Then, when there is a special command,
the Beloved enters the heart. 3
In that extraordinary circumstance,
the bhava that is intuited is never worldly;
it is separate from the concerns of the physical body.

Whatever the difficult circumstance,
never be uncompromising. 4

Without being obstinate,
maintain a keen sense of awareness in all situations,
and recognize what is dharma and what is not.
This is my explanation of wisdom,
and now I will speak of perseverance. 5

त्रिदुःख-सहनं धैर्यम् आमृतेः सर्वतः सदा।
तक्रवद्-देहवद्-भाव्यं जडवद्-गोपभार्यवत् ॥६॥

triduḥkha-sahanaṃ dhairyam āmṛteḥ sarvataḥ sadā
6 *takravad-dehavad-bhāvyaṃ jaḍavad-gopabhāryavat*

प्रतीकारो यदृच्छातः सिद्धश्चेन्-नाग्रही भवेत्।
भार्यादीनां तथान्येषाम् असतश्चाक्रमं सहेत् ॥७॥

pratīkāro yadṛcchātaḥ siddhaścen-nāgrahī bhavet
7 *bhāryādīnāṃ tathānyeṣām asataścākramaṃ sahet*

स्वयम् इन्द्रिय-कार्याणि काय-वाङ् मनसा त्यजेत्।
अशूरेणाऽपि कर्तव्यं स्वस्यासामर्थ्य-भावनात् ॥८॥

svayam indriya-kāryāṇi kāya-vāṅ manasā tyajet
8 *aśūreṇā'pi kartavyaṃ svasyāsāmarthya-bhāvanāt*

अशक्ये हरिरेवास्ति सर्वम् आश्रयतो भवेत्।
एतत् सहनम् अत्रोक्तम् आश्रयोऽतो निरूप्यते ॥९॥

aśakye harirevāsti sarvam āśrayato bhavet
9 *etat sahanam atroktam āśrayo'to nirūpyate*

Perseverance is to always endure the three types of pain
(mundane, spiritual, and divine) until death.
To accomplish this,
understand the body to be like buttermilk,
which remains unaffected even after
it has been beaten and robbed of its butter.

Also comprehend the spiritual pains of King Bharat,
who underwent three births
before he became enlightened,
as well as the divine pangs of separation from Shri Krishna
that the gopis of Vrindavan experienced. 6

When there is alleviation
and things work out because of his wish,
do not resist the accomplishment.
Endure false attacks from your spouse,
family members, and other people. 7

Sense activities that are not connected to Hari
should be renounced with mind, body, and speech.
Even if one is powerless, renunciation should be done
understanding that the power to do so
is not one's own, but his. 8

In the powerless position,
remember that Hari is everything
and that entirety is attained through refuge.
Thus I have spoken of fortitude,
and now I will introduce the third teaching,
which is refuge in Hari. 9

ऐहिके पारलोके च सर्वथा शरणं हरिः ।
दुःख-हानौ तथा पापे भये कामाद्यपूरणे ॥१०॥

aihike pāraloke ca sarvathā śaraṇaṃ hariḥ
10 *duḥkha-hānau tathā pāpe bhaye kāmādyapūraṇe*

भक्तद्रोहे भक्त्यभावे भक्तैश्चातिक्रमे कृते ।
अशक्ये वा सुशक्ये वा सर्वथा शरणं हरिः ॥११॥

bhaktadrohe bhaktyabhāve bhaktaiścātikrame kṛte
11 *aśakye vā suśakye vā sarvathā śaraṇaṃ hariḥ*

अहङ्कार-कृते चैव पोष्य-पोषण-रक्षणे ।
पोष्यातिक्रमणे चैव तथाऽन्तेवास्यतिक्रमे ॥१२॥

ahaṅkāra-kṛte caiva poṣya-poṣaṇa-rakṣaṇe
12 *poṣyātikramaṇe caiva tathā'ntevāsyatikrame*

अलौकिक-मनःसिद्धौ सर्वार्थे शरणं हरिः ।
एवं चित्ते सदा भाव्यं वाचा च परिकीर्तयेत् ॥१३॥

alaukika-manaḥsiddhau sarvārthe śaraṇaṃ hariḥ
13 *evaṃ citte sadā bhāvyaṃ vācā ca parikīrtayet*

अन्यस्य भजनं तत्र स्वतो-गमनमेव च ।
प्रार्थना कार्यमात्रेऽपि ततोऽन्यत्र विवर्जयेत् ॥१४॥

anyasya bhajanaṃ tatra svato-gamanameva ca
14 *prārthanā kāryamātre'pi tato'nyatra vivarjayet*

In this world, or in any other,
and in every situation, Shri Hari is the refuge.

In pain and loss, in sin or in fear,
in the non-obtainment of the object of desire, 10
in anger towards other bhaktas,
in the absence of devotion,
in the case of other bhaktas
being aggressive with you,
in the powerless state,
as well as in the position of power,
always remember that Shri Hari is the refuge. 11

In the creation of false pride,
in the protection and nourishment
of those who need sustenance,
or in violations from those who are being nourished,
as well as in the transgressions of students 12
or even in the perfection of the divine heart-mind,
always take Hari's refuge in every situation.
Maintain this sensibility firmly in the mind,
and praise it with the voice. 13

It is also forbidden to worship another,
or to pray to another
for any of your work to be done. 14

अविश्वासो न कर्तव्यः सर्वथा बाधकस्तु सः।
ब्रह्मास्त्र-चातकौ भाव्यौ प्राप्तं सेवेत निर्ममः ॥ १५॥

aviśvāso na kartavyaḥ sarvathā bādhakastu saḥ
15 *brahmāstra-cātakau bhāvyau prāptaṃ seveta nirmamaḥ*

यथाकथञ्चित् कार्याणि कुर्याद् उच्चावचान्यपि।
किं वा प्रोक्तेन बहुना शरणं भावयेद् हरिम् ॥ १६॥

yathākathañcit kāryāṇi kuryād uccāvacānyapi
16 *kiṃ vā proktena bahunā śaraṇaṃ bhāvayed harim*

एवम् आश्रयणं प्रोक्तं सर्वेषां सर्वदा हितम्।
कलौ भक्त्यादिमार्गा हि दुःसाध्या इति मे मतिः ॥ १७॥

evam āśrayaṇaṃ proktaṃ sarveṣāṃ sarvadā hitam
17 *kalau bhaktyādimārgā hi duḥsādhyā iti me matiḥ*

॥इति श्रीवल्लभाचार्य-विरचितं विवेकधैर्याश्रय-निरूपणं सम्पूर्णम् ॥

iti śrīvallabhācārya-viracitaṃ
vivekadhairyāśraya-nirūpaṇaṃ sampūrṇam

Never lose faith.
If you do, it will impede your every situation.

Understand lack of faith from the story of Hanuman,
who broke free from the powerful Brahmastra weapon
because his captors lost faith in it.

Understand faith from the tale of
the chataka bird, who forsakes all waters
except the rain drops from certain clouds.

Perform seva, Hari's pleasing worship,
with whatever is obtained
and without false sense of ownership. 15

In all undertakings,
whether they be high or low,
religious or worldly,
maintain the bhava that
"Shri Hari is my refuge." 16

What more is there to say?

Thus I have spoken of refuge in Hari,
which is at all times beneficial to all.

In my opinion, bhakti and other practices
are difficult to perform in this age of struggle,
and therefore, one should take to the path of refuge. 17

Thus ends Viveka Dhairyāśrayaḥ by Shri Vallabhacharya.

कृष्णाश्रयस्तोत्रम्

Kṛṣṇāśraya Stotram

Refuge in Krishna

In this teaching, Shri Vallabhacharya surveys the contrary conditions that prevailed in India some five hundred years ago and advises his followers to seek Shri Krishna's refuge in every circumstance. It was written in Adel for his follower Bula Mishra in about 1514 CE. Bhaktas daily recite this text while in seva to help establish their total shelter in Shri Krishna.

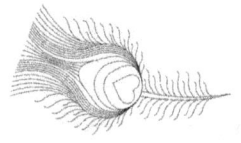

सर्वमार्गेषु नष्टेषु कलौ च खलधर्मिणि ।
पाषण्डप्रचुरे लोके कृष्ण एव गतिर्मम ॥ १ ॥

sarvamārgeṣu naṣṭeṣu kalau ca khaladharmiṇi
1 *pāṣaṇḍapracure loke kṛṣṇa eva gatirmama*

म्लेच्छाक्रान्तेषु देशेषु पापैक-निलयेषु च ।
सत्पीडा-व्यग्र-लोकेषु कृष्ण एव गतिर्मम ॥ २ ॥

mlecchākrānteṣu deśeṣu pāpaika-nilayeṣu ca
2 *satpīḍā-vyagra-lokeṣu kṛṣṇa eva gatirmama*

गङ्गादि-तीर्थ-वर्येषु दुष्टैर् एवावृतेष्विह ।
तिरोहिताधिदैवेषु कृष्ण एव गतिर्मम ॥ ३ ॥

gaṅgādi-tīrtha-varyeṣu duṣṭair evāvṛteṣviha
3 *tirohitādhidaiveṣu kṛṣṇa eva gatirmama*

अहङ्कार-विमूढेषु सत्सु पापानुवर्तिषु ।
लाभ-पूजार्थ-यत्नेषु कृष्ण एव गतिर्मम ॥ ४ ॥

ahaṅkāra-vimūḍheṣu satsu pāpānuvartiṣu
4 *lābha-pūjārtha-yatneṣu kṛṣṇa eva gatirmama*

All proper paths have been destroyed
in this age of struggle.
The practitioners of dharma
have become wicked,
and hypocrisy is rampant.
Krishna alone is my refuge. 1

India has been invaded by barbarians
and has become an abode full of impurity,
where people are disturbed because of
the suffering of the pure hearted ones.
Krishna alone is my refuge. 2

The Ganga and other holy places
have been surrounded by wicked people.
The presiding devas have hidden themselves.
Krishna alone is my refuge. 3

Even pious people
are bewildered by their own egos
and follow sinful activity.
The worship they perform is for personal gain.
Krishna alone is my refuge. 4

अपरि-ज्ञान-नष्टेषु मंत्रेष्वव्रत-योगिषु।
तिरोहितार्थ-देवेषु कृष्ण एव गतिर्मम ॥५॥

apari-jñāna-naṣṭeṣu mantreṣvavrata-yogiṣu
5 *tirohitārtha-deveṣu kṛṣṇa eva gatirmama*

नाना-वाद-विनष्टेषु सर्व-कर्म-व्रतादिषु।
पाषण्डैक-प्रयत्नेषु कृष्ण एव गतिर्मम ॥६॥

nānā-vāda-vinaṣṭeṣu sarva-karma-vratādiṣu
6 *pāṣaṇḍaika-prayatneṣu kṛṣṇa eva gatirmama*

अजामिलादि-दोषाणां नाशकोऽनुभवे स्थितः।
ज्ञापिताऽखिल-माहात्म्यः कृष्ण एव गतिर्मम ॥७॥

ajāmilādi-doṣāṇāṃ nāśako'nubhave sthitaḥ
7 *jñāpitā'khila-māhātmyaḥ kṛṣṇa eva gatirmama*

प्राकृताः सकला देवा गणितानन्दकं बृहत्।
पूर्णानन्दो हरिस् तस्मात् कृष्ण एव गतिर्मम ॥८॥

prākṛtāḥ sakalā devā gaṇitānandakaṃ bṛhat
8 *pūrṇānando haris tasmāt kṛṣṇa eva gatirmama*

True knowledge has been lost,
along with the proper use of
mantras, fasts, and yoga.
Inner meanings and the devas
have all become concealed.
Krishna alone is my refuge. 5

Many different false teachings
have destroyed all the pious karmas
and religious observances.
People's spiritual undertakings
are filled with hypocrisy.
Krishna alone is my refuge. 6

Bhaktas know him as the one
who removed the impurities
of sinners like Ajamila and others.
He has thus revealed his total eminence.
Krishna alone is my refuge. 7

All the gods are material.
Even formless Brahman's bliss is qualified.
Hari alone is replete with perfect joy.
Krishna alone is my refuge. 8

विवेक-धैर्य-भक्त्यादि-रहितस्य विशेषतः ।
पापासक्तस्य दीनस्य कृष्ण एव गतिर्मम ॥ ९ ॥

viveka-dhairya-bhaktyādi-rahitasya viśeṣataḥ
9 *pāpāsaktasya dīnasya kṛṣṇa eva gatirmama*

सर्व-सामर्थ्य-सहितः सर्वत्रैवाखिलार्थकृत् ।
शरणस्थ-समुद्धारं कृष्णं विज्ञापयाम्यहम् ॥ १० ॥

sarva-sāmarthya-sahitaḥ sarvatraivākhilārthakṛt
10 *śaraṇastha-samuddhāraṃ kṛṣṇaṃ vijñāpayāmyaham*

कृष्णाश्रयम् इदं स्तोत्रं यः पठेत् कृष्ण-सन्निधौ ।
तस्याश्रयो भवेत् कृष्ण इति श्रीवल्लभोऽब्रवीत् ॥ ११ ॥

kṛṣṇāśrayam idaṃ stotraṃ yaḥ paṭhet kṛṣṇa-sannidhau
11 *tasyāśrayo bhavet kṛṣṇa iti śrīvallabho'bravīt*

॥ इति श्रीवल्लभाचार्य-विरचितं कृष्णाश्रय-स्तोत्रं सम्पूर्णम् ॥
iti śrīvallabhācārya-viracitaṃ kṛṣṇāśraya-stotraṃ sampūrṇam

I am totally devoid of
wisdom, patience, devotion, and other virtues.
I am attached to sin, but I am humble.
Krishna alone is my refuge. 9

I pray to you, Shri Krishna,
who are full of all powers and
fulfill the bhaktas' desires in every circumstance.
You uplift those who take your shelter. 10

Whoever recites this prayer
in Shri Krishna's proximity attains his shelter.
So says Shri Vallabha. 11

Thus ends Kṛṣṇāśraya Stotram by Shri Vallabhacharya.

चतुःश्लोकी

Catuḥ Ślokī

Four Verses

Shri Vallabhacharya gave this short teaching to Rana Vyasa and Bhagavandas Sanchora around 1523 CE in Kashi. Each verse of the text gives a grace filled interpretation of one of the four pursuits of life: *dharma*, wealth (*artha*), desire (*kāma*), and liberation (*mokṣa*). His worship is our dharma, and our wealth is Shri Krishna himself. Our desires are fulfilled when he lives in our hearts, and to always serve and remember him is liberation.

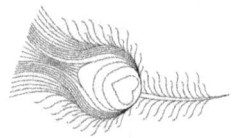

सर्वदा सर्वभावेन भजनीयो व्रजाधिपः ।
स्वस्यायमेव धर्मो हि नान्यः क्वापि कदाचन ॥ १ ॥

sarvadā sarvabhāvena bhajanīyo vrajādhipaḥ
1 *svasyāyameva dharmo hi nānyaḥ kvāpi kadācana*

एवं सदा स्म कर्तव्यं स्वयमेव करिष्यति ।
प्रभुः सर्वसमर्थो हि ततो निश्चिन्ततां व्रजेत् ॥ २ ॥

evaṃ sadā sma kartavyaṃ svayameva kariṣyati
2 *prabhuḥ sarvasamartho hi tato niścintatāṃ vrajet*

यदि श्रीगोकुलाधीशो धृतः सर्वात्मना हृदि ।
ततः किम् अपरं ब्रूहि लौकिकैर् वैदिकैर् अपि ॥ ३ ॥

yadi śrīgokulādhīśo dhṛtaḥ sarvātmanā hṛdi
3 *tataḥ kim aparaṃ brūhi laukikair vaidikair api*

अतः सर्वात्मना शश्वद् गोकुलेश्वर-पादयोः ।
स्मरणं भजनं चाऽपि न त्याज्यम् इति मे मतिः ॥ ४ ॥

ataḥ sarvātmanā śaśvad gokuleśvara-pādayoḥ
4 *smaraṇaṃ bhajanaṃ cā'pi na tyājyam iti me matiḥ*

॥इति श्रीवल्लभाचार्य-विरचिता चतुःश्लोकी सम्पूर्णा ॥
iti śrīvallabhācārya-viracitā catuḥślokī sampūrṇā

The Lord of Vraja is always worthy of
worship with every bhava.
That is your only dharma.
There is never another one anywhere. 1

This is always your duty.
Shri Krishna himself will do the rest,
for he is all-powerful.
Therefore, go and live without concern. 2

If the Lord of Gokul, Shri Krishna,
fills your heart with total love,
nothing promised in the world or in the Vedas
can exceed that. 3

And so, always maintain
this state of total love for Shri Krishna.
Serve and remember his lotus feet.
My belief is that this view
should never be forsaken. 4

Thus ends Catuḥ Ślokī by Shri Vallabhacharya.

भक्तिवर्धिनी

Bhakti Vardhinī

How to Increase Devotion

Shri Vallabhacharya gave this teaching to Purushottam Joshi in about 1496 CE in Gujarat. It is an essential bhakti empowerment and offers devotional solutions for various situations that might arise in a practitioner's life. This text explains how to attain love for Shri Krishna (*prema*), divine attachment (*āsakti*), and ultimately addiction to him (*vyasana*).

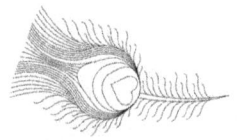

यथा भक्तिः प्रवृद्धा स्यात् तथोपायो निरूप्यते।
बीजभावे दृढे तु स्यात् त्यागाच्छ्रवण-कीर्तनात् ॥१॥

yathā bhaktiḥ pravṛddhā syāt tathopāyo nirūpyate
1 *bījabhāve dṛḍhe tu syāt tyāgācchravaṇa-kīrtanāt*

बीजदार्ढ्य-प्रकारस्तु गृहे स्थित्वा स्वधर्मतः।
अव्यावृत्तो भजेत् कृष्णं पूजया श्रवणादिभिः ॥२॥

bījadārḍhya-prakārastu gṛhe sthitvā svadharmataḥ
2 *avyāvṛtto bhajet kṛṣṇaṃ pūjayā śravaṇādibhiḥ*

व्यावृत्तोऽपि हरौ चित्तं श्रवणादौ यतेत् सदा।
ततः प्रेम तथाऽसक्तिर्-व्यसनं च यदा भवेत् ॥३॥

vyāvṛtto'pi harau cittaṃ śravaṇādau yatet sadā
3 *tataḥ prema tathā'saktir-vyasanaṃ ca yadā bhavet*

I will now explain how to increase bhakti.
Once the seed of devotion has become firm,
nourish it by renouncing what is unrelated,
listening to devotional subjects,
and singing his praises. 1

The way to strengthen the seed of blessed devotion
is to reside at home and to follow your own dharma.
If you are free from all other occupations,
worship Shri Krishna lovingly.
Serve him with song, perform devotional listening,
and undertake other exalted activities. 2

If you do have worldly obligations,
fix the mind on Hari by always listening to his praises,
or by engaging in other devotional activities.
Then, the blessed states of love, attachment,
and finally addiction to the blessed one will follow. 3

बीजं तद् उच्यते शास्त्रे दृढं यन् नाऽपि नश्यति ।
स्नेहाद् रागविनाशः स्याद् आसक्त्या स्याद् गृहारुचिः ॥४॥

bījaṃ tad ucyate śāstre dṛḍhaṃ yan nā'pi naśyati
4 *snehād rāgavināśaḥ syād āsaktyā syād gṛhāruciḥ*

गृहस्थानां बाधकत्वम् अनात्मत्वं च भासते ।
यदा स्याद् व्यसनं कृष्णे कृतार्थः स्यात् तदैव हि ॥५॥

gṛhasthānāṃ bādhakatvam anātmatvaṃ ca bhāsate
5 *yadā syād vyasanaṃ kṛṣṇe kṛtārthaḥ syāt tadaiva hi*

तादृशस्याऽपि सततं गेहस्थानं विनाशकम् ।
त्यागं कृत्वा यतेद् यस्तु तदर्थार्थैकमानसः ॥६॥

tādṛśasyā'pi satataṃ gehasthānaṃ vināśakam
6 *tyāgaṃ kṛtvā yated yastu tadarthārthaikamānasaḥ*

लभते सुदृढां भक्तिं सर्वतोऽप्यधिकां पराम् ।
त्यागे बाधकभूयस्त्वं दुःसंसर्गात् तथाऽन्नतः ॥७॥

labhate sudṛḍhāṃ bhaktiṃ sarvato'pyadhikāṃ parām
7 *tyāge bādhakabhūyastvaṃ duḥsaṃsargāt tathā'nnataḥ*

In the blessed state of addiction,
the devotional seed becomes perfectly established.
The sacred writings tell us that
it can then never be destroyed.

Divine love removes worldly hankering.

When one becomes attached to the Beloved,
one loses all taste for the worldly home 4
and sees it as unconnected to one's true self.

When the bhakta becomes
totally addicted to Shri Krishna
and can no longer live without him,
that blessed one has attained devotional excellence. 5

The devotionally accomplished soul
will always experience the worldly home
as destructive to devotion.
Renunciation is only so that
one can focus the mind and heart. 6

The attainment of firm devotion
is superior to and beyond anything else.

If there is premature renunciation,
one will encounter many obstructions, such as
bad association and unoffered, impure food. 7

अतः स्थेयं हरिस्थाने तदीयैः सह तत्परैः ।
अदूरे विप्रकर्षे वा यथा चित्तं न दुष्यति ॥८॥

ataḥ stheyaṃ haristhāne tadīyaiḥ saha tatparaiḥ
8 *adūre viprakarṣe vā yathā cittaṃ na duṣyati*

सेवायां वा कथायां वा यस्याऽसक्तिर् दृढा भवेत् ।
यावज्जीवं तस्य नाशो न क्वाऽपीति मतिर् मम ॥९॥

sevāyāṃ vā kathāyāṃ vā yasyā'saktir dṛḍhā bhavet
9 *yāvajjīvaṃ tasya nāśo na kvā'pīti matir mama*

बाधसम्भावनायां तु नैकान्ते वास इष्यते ।
हरिस्तु सर्वतो रक्षां करिष्यति न संशयः ॥१०॥

bādhasambhāvanāyāṃ tu naikānte vāsa iṣyate
10 *haristu sarvato rakṣāṃ kariṣyati na saṃśayaḥ*

इत्येवं भगवच्छास्त्रं गूढतत्त्वं निरूपितम् ।
य एतत् समधीयीत तस्यापि स्याद् दृढा रतिः ॥११॥

ityevaṃ bhagavacchāstraṃ gūḍhatattvaṃ nirūpitam
11 *ya etat samadhīyīta tasyāpi syād dṛḍhā ratiḥ*

॥इति श्रीवल्लभाचार्य-विरचिता भक्तिवर्धिनी सम्पूर्णा ॥
iti śrīvallabhācārya-viracitā bhaktivardhinī sampūrṇā

And so, one should
live in a place that is sacred to Shri Hari and
focus on having association with other bhaktas
who have become Hari's dear ones.

One should maintain a balance
between living near other bhaktas
but keeping a reasonable distance, so that
the mind will never experience any negativity. 8

If one is attached to Shri Krishna's seva, or to
hearing and reciting his names, stories and teachings,
I believe that as long as that bhakta lives,
her devotion will never be destroyed. 9

One should not live in isolation,
because of the possibility of obstructions.
Without a doubt,
Hari will protect the bhakta in every way. 10

And so I have revealed
the secret essence of the blessed Lord's teachings.
Those who grasp them will have firm devotion. 11

Thus ends Bhakti Vardhinī by Shri Vallabhacharya.

जलभेदः

Jala Bhedaḥ

Differences in Waters

In this unique teaching, Shri Vallabhacharya gives insight into the different natures of people who speak and sing about God, and then he compares them to various types of water. Reciters, like water, have many different flavors and attributes. When you can correctly judge what you are listening to, the ability to imbibe only pure teachings is greatly increased.

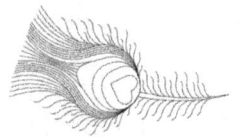

नमस्कृत्य हरिं वक्ष्ये तद्गुणानां विभेदकान् ।
भावान् विंशतिधा भिन्नान् सर्व-सन्देह-वारकान् ॥ १॥

namaskṛtya hariṃ vakṣye tadguṇānāṃ vibhedakān
1 *bhāvān viṃśatidhā bhinnān sarva-sandeha-vārakān*

गुणभेदास्तु तावन्तो यावन्तो हि जले मताः ।
गायकाः कूपसङ्काशा गन्धर्वा इति विश्रुताः ॥ २॥

guṇabhedāstu tāvanto yāvanto hi jale matāḥ
2 *gāyakāḥ kūpasaṅkāśā gandharvā iti viśrutāḥ*

कूपभेदास्तु यावन्तस् तावन्तस्तेऽपि सम्मताः ।
कुल्याः पौराणिकाः प्रोक्ताः पारम्पर्ययुता भुवि ॥ ३॥

kūpabhedāstu yāvantas tāvantaste'pi sammatāḥ
3 *kulyāḥ paurāṇikāḥ proktāḥ pāramparyayutā bhuvi*

क्षेत्र-प्रविष्टास् ते चाऽपि संसारोत्पत्ति-हेतवः ।
वेश्यादि-सहिता मत्ता गायका गर्त-सञ्ज्ञिताः ॥ ४॥

kṣetra-praviṣṭās te cā'pi saṃsārotpatti-hetavaḥ
4 *veśyādi-sahitā mattā gāyakā garta-sañjñitāḥ*

Having bowed to Hari,
I will now remove all doubts
with my explanation of his different attributes,
by describing the nature of
twenty different types of speakers. 1

There are as many different types of speakers
as there are kinds of water.
The first type of singer (*gayaka*)
I will mention are known in scriptures as
gandharvas—celestial singers.
They resemble wells. 2
Like wells, they are of various types:
some are sweet, while others are brackish.

Then there are the reciters of Puranic lore.
It is their family tradition. 3
I consider them to be like canals.
When their waters are diverted into fields,
their flow creates worldliness.

The next type of singers are those
who are intoxicated and associate with prostitutes.
They are like stagnant water holes. 4

जलार्थमेव गर्तास्तु नीचा गानोपजीविनः ।
हृदास्तु पण्डिताः प्रोक्ता भगवच्छास्त्र-तत्पराः ॥५॥

jalārthameva gartāstu nīcā gānopajīvinaḥ
5 *hṛdāstu paṇḍitāḥ proktā bhagavacchāstra-tatparāḥ*

सन्देह-वारकास् तत्र सूदा गम्भीर-मानसाः ।
सरः कमल-सम्पूर्णाः प्रेमयुक्तास् तथा बुधाः ॥६॥

sandeha-vārakās tatra sūdā gambhīra-mānasāḥ
6 *saraḥ kamala-sampūrṇāḥ premayuktās tathā budhāḥ*

अल्पश्रुताः प्रेमयुक्ता वेशन्ताः परिकीर्तिताः ।
कर्मशुद्धाः पल्वलानि तथाल्प-श्रुत-भक्तयः ॥७॥

alpaśrutāḥ premayuktā veśantāḥ parikīrtitāḥ
7 *karmaśuddhāḥ palvalāni tathālpa-śruta-bhaktayaḥ*

योग-ध्यानादि-संयुक्ता गुणा वर्ष्याः प्रकीर्तिताः ।
तपो-ज्ञानादि-भावेन स्वेदजास्तु प्रकीर्तिताः ॥८॥

yoga-dhyānādi-saṃyuktā guṇā varṣyāḥ prakīrtitāḥ
8 *tapo-jñānādi-bhāvena svedajāstu prakīrtitāḥ*

Lowly singers who only recite for money
are like sewer water.

Then there are pundits who are
always intent upon reciting the Lord's glories
as revealed in the *Shrimad Bhagavatam*. 5
They are like deep water.

Then there are some speakers
who can remove the doubts of others.
They have profound minds and hearts.
I compare them to pure, sweet, nectar-like water.

Those who are brilliant and full of love are like
lakes brimming with lotuses. 6

Those who have a little bit of knowledge and love,
I call ponds.

Others who perform good deeds but have
very limited devotion and understanding
are like water holes. 7

I refer to those who perform
yoga, meditation, and other related practices
as rainwater.

Those who trouble themselves with austerities
and have a bit of knowledge
are like perspiration. 8

अलौकिकेन ज्ञानेन ये तु प्रोक्ता हरेर् गुणाः ।
कादाचित्काः शब्दगम्याः पतच्छब्दाः प्रकीर्तिताः ॥९॥

alaukikena jñānena ye tu proktā harer guṇāḥ
9 *kādācitkāḥ śabdagamyāḥ patacchabdāḥ prakīrtitāḥ*

देवाद्युपासनोद्भूताः पृष्वा भूमेर्-इवोद्गताः ।
साधनादि-प्रकारेण नवधा भक्तिमार्गतः ॥१०॥

devādyupāsanodbhūtāḥ pṛṣvā bhūmer-ivodgatāḥ
10 *sādhanādi-prakāreṇa navadhā bhaktimārgataḥ*

प्रेमपूर्त्या स्फुरद्धर्माः स्यन्दमानाः प्रकीर्तिताः ।
यादृशास्-तादृशाः प्रोक्ता वृद्धि-क्षय-विवर्जिताः ॥११॥

premapūrtyā sphuraddharmāḥ syandamānāḥ prakīrtitāḥ
11 *yādṛśās-tādṛśāḥ proktā vṛddhi-kṣaya-vivarjitāḥ*

स्थावरास् ते समाख्याता मर्यादैक-प्रतिष्ठिताः ।
अनेक-जन्म-संसिद्धा जन्म-प्रभृति सर्वदा ॥१२॥

sthāvarās te samākhyātā maryādaika-pratiṣṭhitāḥ
12 *aneka-janma-saṃsiddhā janma-prabhṛti sarvadā*

सङ्गादि-गुण-दोषाभ्यां वृद्धि-क्षय-युता भुवि ।
निरन्तरोद्गमयुता नद्यस् ते परिकीर्तिताः ॥१३॥

saṅgādi-guṇa-doṣābhyāṃ vṛddhi-kṣaya-yutā bhuvi
13 *nirantarodgamayutā nadyas te parikīrtitāḥ*

Sometimes you find a speaker with divine insight
who speaks of Hari's attributes.
That person's words are like a waterfall. 9

Those who worship the material devas are
like dew that appears to have sprung from the earth.

By various practices, including
the nine-fold devotional path (*navadhā bhakti*), 10
a person can become full of love and
bright with God's dharma.
I call such a blessed one a flowing spring.

Those similar to the speakers I have just mentioned,
who neither grow nor shrink, 11
but remain firmly situated on the path of law,
I compare to still water.

Then there are those who have received
the fruits of their good and bad actions for lifetimes. 12
In this world they find both good and bad association,
from which they sometimes profit and sometimes lose.
Such souls are always on the move.
I call them streams. 13

एतादृशाः स्वतन्त्राश् चेत् सिन्धवः परिकीर्तिताः ।
पूर्णा भगवदीया ये शेष-व्यासाग्नि-मारुताः ॥ १४॥

etādṛśāḥ svatantrāś cet sindhavaḥ parikīrtitāḥ
14 *pūrṇā bhagavadīyā ye śeṣa-vyāsāgni-mārutāḥ*

जड-नारद-मैत्राद्यास् ते समुद्राः प्रकीर्तिताः ।
लोक-वेद-गुणैर् मिश्र-भावेनैके हरेर् गुणान् ॥ १५॥

jaḍa-nārada-maitrādyās te samudrāḥ prakīrtitāḥ
15 *loka-veda-guṇair miśra-bhāvenaike harer guṇān*

वर्णयन्ति समुद्रास् ते क्षाराद्याः षट् प्रकीर्तिताः ।
गुणातीततया शुद्धान् सच्चिदानन्द-रूपिणः ॥ १६॥

varṇayanti samudrās te kṣārādyāḥ ṣaṭ prakīrtitāḥ
16 *guṇātītatayā śuddhān saccidānanda-rūpiṇaḥ*

सर्वानेव गुणान् विष्णोर् वर्णयन्ति विचक्षणाः ।
तेऽमृतोदाः समाख्यातास् तद् वाक् पानं सुदुर्लभम् ॥ १७॥

sarvāneva guṇān viṣṇor varṇayanti vicakṣaṇāḥ
17 *te'mṛtodāḥ samākhyātās tad vāk pānaṃ sudurlabham*

तादृशानां क्वचिद् वाक्यं दूतानामिव वर्णितम् ।
अजामिलाकर्णनवद् बिन्दुपानं प्रकीर्तितम् ॥ १८॥

tādṛśānāṃ kvacid vākyaṃ dūtānāmiva varṇitam
18 *ajāmilākarṇanavad bindupānaṃ prakīrtitam*

Similar to them are the singers
who are free of binding karmas.
They are large rivers, like the Indus.

Then there are those who are great devotees,
like Shesha, Vyasa, Vayu, 14
Jadabharata, Narada, Maitreya, and other sages.
I refer to them all as oceans.
These ocean-like singers
glorify blessed Hari with different moods.
Their praise is mixed
with the virtues of the world and Vedas. 15
They are named after the six oceans of
salt, spirit, ghee,
milk, yoghurt, and nectar.

The wise bhaktas praise Hari as pure,
beyond the material realms
and full of truth, consciousness, and bliss. 16
They praise all of his divine virtues.
Such speakers are like an ocean of nectar.
It is rare to hear their words. 17

Sometimes we can hear
the words of Vishnu's messengers.
Ajamila heard them when
the messengers of death tried to take him away.
Their words are like drops of nectar. 18

रागाज्ञानादि-भावानां सर्वथा नाशनं यदा ।
तदा लेहनम् इत्युक्तं स्वानन्दोद्गम-कारणम् ॥१९॥

rāgājñānādi-bhāvānāṃ sarvathā nāśanaṃ yadā
19 *tadā lehanam ityuktaṃ svānandodgama-kāraṇam*

उद्धृतोदक-वत् सर्वे पतितोदक-वत् तथा ।
उक्तातिरिक्त-वाक्यानि फलं चाऽपि तथा ततः ॥२०॥

uddhṛtodaka-vat sarve patitodaka-vat tathā
20 *uktātirikta-vākyāni phalaṃ cā'pi tathā tataḥ*

इति जीवेन्द्रियगता नाना-भावं गता भुवि ।
रूपतः फलतश्चैव गुणा विष्णोर् निरूपिताः ॥२१॥

iti jīvendriyagatā nānā-bhāvaṃ gatā bhuvi
21 *rūpataḥ phalataścaiva guṇā viṣṇor nirūpitāḥ*

॥इति श्रीवल्लभाचार्य-विरचितो जलभेदः सम्पूर्णः ॥
iti śrīvallabhācārya-viracito jalabhedaḥ sampūrṇaḥ

When worldly passion, ignorance,
and other mundane moods are forever destroyed
and one experiences the joy of the inner self,
that I call true taste. 19

Different from all other types of reciters are
the speakers who are like water in a vessel,
or water that has spilled to the ground.
Their speech corresponds to
the type of water vessel
or the place the water has spilled.
They are never exalted speakers. 20

And so the blessed Lord's qualities
have been explained as they arise in this world
and create different states of being
within people's souls and senses.
By using examples of different types of water,
I have revealed the various natures of the speakers
and the rewards which they receive. 21

Thus ends Jala Bhedaḥ by Shri Vallabhacharya.

पञ्चपद्यानि

Pañca Padyāni

Five Lines

The previous teaching, *Differences in Waters*, depicted the various types of speakers. Here we find a description of four categories of listeners. One of the main devotional practices is listening, and Shri Vallabhacharya explains to us the different effects it has upon the bhaktas. The fruit of hearing is comprehension that creates an enlightened response.

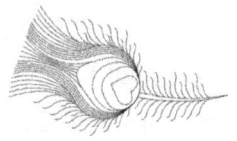

श्रीकृष्णरस-विक्षिप्त-मानसा-रतिवर्जिताः।
अनिर्वृता लोक-वेदे ते मुख्याः श्रवणोत्सुकाः॥१॥

śrīkṛṣṇarasa-vikṣipta-mānasā-rativarjitāḥ
1 *anirvṛtā loka-vede te mukhyāḥ śravaṇotsukāḥ*

विक्लिन्नमनसो ये तु भगवत् स्मृति-विह्वलाः।
अर्थैकनिष्ठास् ते चाऽपि मध्यमाः श्रवणोत्सुकाः॥२॥

viklinnamanaso ye tu bhagavat smṛti-vihvalāḥ
2 *arthaikaniṣṭhās te cā'pi madhyamāḥ śravaṇotsukāḥ*

निःसन्दिग्धं कृष्णतत्त्वं सर्वभावेन ये विदुः।
ते त्वावेशात् तु विकला निरोधाद् वा न चान्यथा॥३॥

niḥsandigdhaṃ kṛṣṇatattvaṃ sarvabhāvena ye viduḥ
3 *te tvāveśāt tu vikalā nirodhād vā na cānyathā*

पूर्णभावेन पूर्णार्थाः कदाचिन् न तु सर्वदा।
अन्यासक्तास् तु ये केचिद् अधमाः परिकीर्तिताः॥४॥

pūrṇabhāvena pūrṇārthāḥ kadācin na tu sarvadā
4 *anyāsaktās tu ye kecid adhamāḥ parikīrtitāḥ*

The preeminent devotional listeners
are those grace filled beings
whose minds and hearts are totally immersed
in Shri Krishna's loving nectar.
They only embrace divine love
and have no taste for worldly or Vedic pleasures. 1

The intermediate group of
devotionally inspired listeners are overwhelmed
when they remember the beloved Lord.
Their hearts are soft,
but they mainly focus on the meaning,
with underlying desire for liberation
or other spiritual fruit. 2

Other listeners know Shri Krishna's essence
beyond a doubt and with all devotional feelings.
They are stricken with devotion
only when possessed by Hari (*āveśa*),
or when they fall under his divine control (*nirodha*),
but not at any other time. 3
They sometimes become full of divine mood
and devotional purpose.
However, this is not their constant state.
They become distracted
by their attachments to worldly things.
They are the least exalted type of devotional listeners. 4

अनन्यमनसो मर्त्या उत्तमाः श्रवणादिषु।
देश-काल-द्रव्य-कर्तृ-मन्त्र-कर्म-प्रकारतः ॥५॥

ananyamanaso martyā uttamāḥ śravaṇādiṣu
5 *deśa-kāla-dravya-kartṛ-mantra-karma-prakārataḥ*

॥इति श्रीवल्लभाचार्य-विरचितानि पञ्चपद्यानि समाप्तानि ॥
iti śrīvallabhācārya-viracitāni pañcapadyāni samāptāni

The most exalted of listeners
on the path of refuge are those
whose mind and heart are one-pointed.
Their focus is never disturbed by conditions of
location, time, wealth,
agency, mantra, or karma. 5

Thus ends Pañca Padyāni by Shri Vallabhacharya.

संन्यासनिर्णयः

Saṃnyāsa Nirṇayaḥ

My Conclusions on Renunciation

What is true renunciation? What should be renounced and when? Shri Vallabhacharya answered these questions for his disciple Narahari Sannyasi in following teaching. This work was composed around 1494 CE in Badrinath. In the path of grace, renunciation is strictly for the experience of divine love and can be done without stepping outside of the home. Thorough study of this text will remove all doubts concerning what to renounce and what to attain.

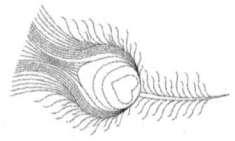

पश्चात्ताप-निर्वृत्त्यर्थं परित्यागो विचार्यते।
स मार्गद्वितये प्रोक्तो भक्तौ ज्ञाने विशेषतः ॥१॥

paścāttāpa-nirvṛttyarthaṃ parityāgo vicāryate
1 *sa mārgadvitaye prokto bhaktau jñāne viśeṣataḥ*

कर्ममार्गे न कर्तव्यः सुतरां कलिकालतः।
अत आदौ भक्तिमार्गे कर्तव्यत्वाद् विचारणा ॥२॥

karmamārge na kartavyaḥ sutarāṃ kalikālataḥ
2 *ata ādau bhaktimārge kartavyatvād vicāraṇā*

श्रवणादि-प्रसिद्ध्यर्थं कर्तव्यश्चेत् स नेष्यते।
सहाय-सङ्गसाध्यत्वात् साधनानां च रक्षणात् ॥३॥

śravaṇādi-prasiddhyarthaṃ kartavyaścet sa neṣyate
3 *sahāya-saṅgasādhyatvāt sādhanānāṃ ca rakṣaṇāt*

In order to remove anxiety,
I will now consider the true nature of renunciation.
Renunciation has been specifically mentioned
in the paths of devotion and knowledge. 1

Renunciation should never be undertaken
in the path of karma,
especially during this current age of struggle.
So I will present my thoughts
on the true nature of renunciation
and how it can be attained according to
the path of loving devotion. 2

If one renounces the world,
hoping to attain perfection
by listening to sacred teachings
and other related spiritual practices,
I say to them that
renunciation of the world is not advisable.
For the practice and protection of devotion,
one needs to take the spiritual assistance of others. 3

अभिमानान् नियोगाच्च तद् धर्मैश्च विरोधतः ।
गृहादेर् बाधकत्वेन साधनार्थं तथा यदि ॥४॥

abhimānān niyogācca tad dharmaiśca virodhataḥ
4 *gṛhāder bādhakatvena sādhanārthaṃ tathā yadi*

अग्रेऽपि तादृशैरेव सङ्गो भवति नान्यथा ।
स्वयं च विषयाक्रान्तः पाषण्डी स्यात्तु कालतः ॥५॥

agre'pi tādṛśaireva saṅgo bhavati nānyathā
5 *svayaṃ ca viṣayākrāntaḥ pāṣaṇḍī syāttu kālataḥ*

विषयाक्रान्त-देहानां नाऽवेशः सर्वदा हरेः ।
अतोऽत्र साधने भक्तौ नैव त्यागः सुखावहः ॥६॥

viṣayākrānta-dehānāṃ nā'veśaḥ sarvadā hareḥ
6 *ato'tra sādhane bhaktau naiva tyāgaḥ sukhāvahaḥ*

विरहानुभवार्थं तु परित्यागः प्रशस्यते ।
स्वीय-बन्ध-निवृत्त्यर्थं वेषः सोऽत्र न चान्यथा ॥७॥

virahānubhavārthaṃ tu parityāgaḥ praśasyate
7 *svīya-bandha-nivṛttyarthaṃ veṣaḥ so'tra na cānyathā*

Furthermore, the practice of renunciation,
especially taking sannyasa (becoming a monk),
can create a false sense of pride.
The sannyasi's restrictions are mostly
contrary to devotional practices.

If one feels that
worldly life is obstructive to devotional life
and therefore renounces the home, 4
let it be known that
the same obstructions found at home
will arise elsewhere, in the form of bad association.
Overcome with mundane hankerings,
that person who renounces the home
thus becomes a hypocrite,
for these are the impure days
of the age of struggle. 5

Know that Hari will never enter the heart
of a person whose body is overcome with worldly desires.
For these reasons, renunciation of the world
will not provide satisfactory results. 6

In the higher states of devotion,
when one yearns to experience
the rapture of separation from the Beloved,
renunciation is praised.
Then, one changes to renunciate's attire only
in order to break ties from worldly family members
and for no other reason. 7

कौण्डिन्यो गोपिकाः प्रोक्ता गुरवः साधनं च तत्।
भावो भावनया सिद्धः साधनं नान्यद् इष्यते ॥८॥

kauṇḍinyo gopikāḥ proktā guravaḥ sādhanaṃ ca tat
8 *bhāvo bhāvanayā siddhaḥ sādhanaṃ nānyad iṣyate*

विकलत्वं तथाऽस्वास्थ्यं प्रकृतिः प्राकृतं न हि।
ज्ञानं गुणाश्च तस्यैवं वर्तमानस्य बाधकाः ॥९॥

vikalatvaṃ tathā'svāsthyaṃ prakṛtiḥ prākṛtaṃ na hi
9 *jñānaṃ guṇāśca tasyaivaṃ vartamānasya bādhakāḥ*

सत्यलोके स्थितिर् ज्ञानात् संन्यासेन विशेषितात्।
भावना साधनं यत्र फलं चाऽपि तथा भवेत् ॥१०॥

satyaloke sthitir jñānāt saṃnyāsena viśeṣitāt
10 *bhāvanā sādhanaṃ yatra phalaṃ cā'pi tathā bhavet*

तादृशाः सत्यलोकादौ तिष्ठन्त्येव न संशयः।
बहिश्चेत् प्रकटः स्वात्मा वह्निवत् प्रविशेद् यदि ॥११॥

tādṛśāḥ satyalokādau tiṣṭhantyeva na saṃśayaḥ
11 *bahiścet prakaṭaḥ svātmā vahnivat praviśed yadi*

Concerning practice,
the guru of lawful devotion is the sage Kaundinya Rishi,
while the grace filled gurus are the gopis of Vrindavan.

The attainment of Shri Krishna
can never be dependent upon any formula.
Shri Krishna, who is perfect bhava,
is attained through precise emulation
of those who have already attained him. 8

The bhakta who has attained
the state of Krishna awareness
is divinely dismayed,
for she can no longer remain without her Beloved.
She is afflicted, yet her condition is not physical.
For such an exalted bhakta,
wisdom and knowledge of Brahman's attributes
are actually obstructions. 9

A renunciate who has distinct knowledge
can go to the highest material sphere of Satya Loka.
Know that the reward attained always corresponds
to the type of worship that was performed. 10

Without a doubt, knowledge-filled renunciates
can remain in Satya Loka.
But for the bhakta, like fire appears from a piece of wood,
the Beloved manifests from the heart
directly before the bhakta
and then re-enters that blessed being. 11

तदैव सकलो बन्धो नाशमेति न चान्यथा ।
गुणास्तु सङ्गराहित्याज् जीवनार्थं भवन्ति हि ॥१२॥

tadaiva sakalo bandho nāśameti na cānyathā
12 *guṇāstu saṅgarāhityāj jīvanārthaṃ bhavanti hi*

भगवान् फलरूपत्वान् नाऽत्र बाधक इष्यते ।
स्वास्थ्यवाक्यं न कर्तव्यं दयालुर् न विरुध्यते ॥१३॥

bhagavān phalarūpatvān nā'tra bādhaka iṣyate
13 *svāsthyavākyaṃ na kartavyaṃ dayālur na virudhyate*

दुर्लभोऽयं परित्यागः प्रेम्णा सिध्यति नान्यथा ।
ज्ञानमार्गे तु संन्यासो द्विविधोऽपि विचारितः ॥१४॥

durlabho'yaṃ parityāgaḥ premṇā sidhyati nānyathā
14 *jñānamārge tu saṃnyāso dvividho'pi vicāritaḥ*

ज्ञानार्थम् उत्तराङ्गं च सिद्धिर् जन्मशतैः परम् ।
ज्ञानं च साधनापेक्षं यज्ञादिश्रवणान् मतम् ॥१५॥

jñānārtham uttarāṅgaṃ ca siddhir janmaśataiḥ param
15 *jñānaṃ ca sādhanāpekṣaṃ yajñādiśravaṇān matam*

This is really the only way that
the bhakta's obstructions are overcome.
The bhakta who does not have
the blessed Lord directly in front of her
maintains her life by feeling his virtues. 12

The blessed Lord himself is the reward.
He does not wish to obstruct his bhakta
by giving her mere words of encouragement
that could actually diminish
the intensity of the devotional experience.
In this divine fashion,
his kindness is not compromised. 13
This type of renunciation is rare
and is attained only through love.

In the path of knowledge,
two kinds of renunciation have been spoken about. 14
One type of person
practices renunciation to attain knowledge.
The superior adept
resorts to renunciation after knowledge has arisen.

In the first type of renunciation,
it takes hundreds of births to attain perfection.
We also hear from the Vedas that
for this knowledge to arise,
sacrifices and other Vedic practices are necessary. 15

अतः कलौ स संन्यासः पश्चात्तापाय नान्यथा।
पाषण्डित्वं भवेच्चाऽपि तस्माज्ज्ञाने न संन्यसेत्॥१६॥

ataḥ kalau sa saṃnyāsaḥ paścāttāpāya nānyathā
16 *pāṣaṇḍitvaṃ bhaveccā'pi tasmājjñāne na saṃnyaset*

सुतरां कलिदोषाणां प्रबलत्वाद् इति स्थितिम्।
भक्तिमार्गेऽपि चेद् दोषस् तदा किं कार्यमुच्यते॥१७॥

sutarāṃ kalidoṣāṇāṃ prabalatvād iti sthitim
17 *bhaktimārge'pi ced doṣas tadā kiṃ kāryamucyate*

अत्रारम्भे न नाशः स्याद् दृष्टान्तस्याप्यभावतः।
स्वास्थ्यहेतोः परित्यागाद् बाधः केनाऽस्य सम्भवेत्॥१८॥

atrārambhe na nāśaḥ syād dṛṣṭāntasyāpyabhāvataḥ
18 *svāsthyahetoḥ parityāgād bādhaḥ kenā'sya sambhavet*

हरिर् अत्र न शक्नोति कर्तुं बाधां कुतोऽपरे।
अन्यथा मातरो बालान् न स्तन्यैः पुपुषुः क्वचित्॥१९॥

harir atra na śaknoti kartuṃ bādhāṃ kuto'pare
19 *anyathā mātaro bālān na stanyaiḥ pupuṣuḥ kvacit*

And so, in this age of struggle,
renunciation only creates regret and breeds hypocrisy.
Therefore, do not renounce
along the lines of the path of knowledge, 16
especially during this age of Kali,
a time when impurities are very powerful.

If the impurities of the Kali Yuga
arise in the practice of devotion,
then what should be done? 17

The answer is that in the path of devotion,
from the very beginning, there can never be any ruin.
Not a single example of such an occurrence can be found.

When the bhakta has renounced her worldly well-being
to delve into the depths of inner renunciation,
what obstruction could ever arise
for such a blessed one? 18
If Shri Hari himself cannot impede her,
for that would be like a mother
refusing to feed her own child,
then how could there be any other hindrance? 19

ज्ञानिनामपि वाक्येन न भक्तं मोहयिष्यति।
आत्मप्रदः प्रियश्चाऽपि किमर्थं मोहयिष्यति ॥२०॥

jñānināmapi vākyena na bhaktaṃ mohayiṣyati
20 *ātmapradaḥ priyaścā'pi kimarthaṃ mohayiṣyati*

तस्मादुक्त-प्रकारेण परित्यागो विधीयताम्।
अन्यथा भ्रश्यते स्वार्थाद् इति मे निश्चिता मतिः ॥२१॥

tasmādukta-prakāreṇa parityāgo vidhīyatām
21 *anyathā bhraśyate svārthād iti me niścitā matiḥ*

इति कृष्ण-प्रसादेन वल्लभेन विनिश्चितम्।
संन्यासवरणं भक्तावन्यथा पतितो भवेत् ॥२२॥

iti kṛṣṇa-prasādena vallabhena viniścitam
22 *saṃnyāsavaraṇaṃ bhaktāvanyathā patito bhavet*

॥इति श्रीवल्लभाचार्य-विरचितः संन्यासनिर्णयः सम्पूर्णः॥
iti śrīvallabhācārya-viracitaḥ saṃnyāsanirṇayaḥ sampūrṇaḥ

The words of people
who follow the path of knowledge
will never bewilder the bhakta.
Why would Shri Hari confuse his bhaktas,
who love him so much
and to whom he has given his very self? 20

Therefore, bhaktas should only renounce
along the devotional path I have narrated.
Anyone who becomes a renunciate
for his own selfish benefit
becomes corrupted in the process.
This is my firm opinion. 21

In this way, with the grace of Shri Krishna,
I, Vallabha, have without a doubt decided
that one should choose
the devotional type of renunciation.
Otherwise, the practitioner
will fall from her purpose. 22

Thus ends Saṃnyāsa Nirṇayaḥ by Shri Vallabhacharya.

निरोधलक्षणम्

Nirodha Lakṣaṇam

Nirodha, Bound by Hari

Shri Vallabhacharya's explanation of nirodha does not follow the traditional yogic definition, which is "to control the wandering tendencies of the senses." Nirodha has to do with our relationship with God. It arises when a bhakta falls under his control and simply forgets everything except her relationship with him. In the blessed state of nirodha, the bhakta is bound by his cords of love and is possessed by his continual presence. In this text, originally written for Raja and Madhav Dube in about 1510 CE, the master prays for nirodha, achieves it, and also explains how to attain it.

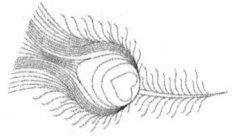

यच्च दुःखं यशोदाया नन्दादीनां च गोकुले।
गोपिकानां तु यद् दुःखं तद् दुःखं स्यान्मम क्वचित्॥१॥

yacca duḥkhaṃ yaśodāyā nandādīnāṃ ca gokule
1 *gopikānāṃ tu yad duḥkhaṃ tad duḥkhaṃ syānmama kvacit*

गोकुले गोपिकानां च सर्वेषां व्रजवासिनाम्।
यत् सुखं समभूत् तन्मे भगवान् किं विधास्यति॥२॥

gokule gopikānāṃ ca sarveṣāṃ vrajavāsinām
2 *yat sukhaṃ samabhūt tanme bhagavān kiṃ vidhāsyati*

उद्धवागमने जात उत्सवः सुमहान् यथा।
वृन्दावने गोकुले वा तथा मे मनसि क्वचित्॥३॥

uddhavāgamane jāta utsavaḥ sumahān yathā
3 *vṛndāvane gokule vā tathā me manasi kvacit*

महतां कृपया यावद् भगवान् दययिष्यति।
तावद् आनन्दसन्दोहः कीर्त्यमानः सुखाय हि॥४॥

mahatāṃ kṛpayā yāvad bhagavān dayayiṣyati
4 *tāvad ānandasandohaḥ kīrtyamānaḥ sukhāya hi*

महतां कृपया यद्वत् कीर्तनं सुखदं सदा।
न तथा लौकिकानां तु स्निग्ध-भोजन-रूक्ष-वत्॥५॥

mahatāṃ kṛpayā yadvat kīrtanaṃ sukhadaṃ sadā
5 *na tathā laukikānāṃ tu snigdha-bhojana-rūkṣa-vat*

When may I experience
that rapture of divine affliction
that struck Shri Krishna's mother Yashoda,
his father Nanda, as well as the gopis
and the other Gokul bhaktas? 1

When will the beloved Lord
give me the joy that the gopis of Gokul and
all the residents of Vraja experienced? 2

When will my heart feel
the great celebration that took place
when Uddhava arrived in Vrindavan and Gokul? 3

As soon as the favor
of the great devotional beings prevails,
the blessed Lord will shower his mercy.
Until then, the singing of his abundant bliss
affords his bhaktas joy. 4

The blessings of the great bhaktas
always produce blissful praise in the singers.
Their songs are not at all
like the tunes of worldly people;
that would be like comparing a rich, delicious meal
to stale, dry food. 5

गुणगाने सुखावाप्तिर् गोविन्दस्य प्रजायते ।
यथा तथा शुकादीनां नैवात्मनि कुतोऽन्यतः ॥६॥

guṇagāne sukhāvāptir govindasya prajāyate
6 *yathā tathā śukādīnāṃ naivātmani kuto'nyataḥ*

क्लिश्यमानान् जनान् दृष्ट्वा कृपायुक्तो यदा भवेत् ।
तदा सर्वं सदानन्दं हृदिस्थं निर्गतं बहिः ॥७॥

kliśyamānān janān dṛṣṭvā kṛpāyukto yadā bhavet
7 *tadā sarvaṃ sadānandaṃ hṛdisthaṃ nirgataṃ bahiḥ*

सर्वानन्दमयस्याऽपि कृपानन्दः सुदुर्लभः ।
हृद्गतः स्वगुणान् श्रुत्वा पूर्णः प्लावयते जनान् ॥८॥

sarvānandamayasyā'pi kṛpānandaḥ sudurlabhaḥ
8 *hṛdgataḥ svaguṇān śrutvā pūrṇaḥ plāvayate janān*

तस्मात् सर्वं परित्यज्य निरुद्धैः सर्वदा गुणाः ।
सदानन्दपरैर् गेयाः सच्चिदानन्दता ततः ॥९॥

tasmāt sarvaṃ parityajya niruddhaiḥ sarvadā guṇāḥ
9 *sadānandaparair geyāḥ saccidānandatā tataḥ*

When the pleasures that arise
from singing the praises of Govinda
are not known even by Shri Sukadeva and others
who are established in self-realization,
then how could they arise in any other place? 6

Yet, when the Beloved sees
the divine affliction of his own souls,
he becomes full of compassion.
Then Shri Hari, who is always joyful,
manifests from their hearts
directly before them. 7

The bliss of his grace is even rarer than
the joy of his omnipresent form.
When Shri Krishna,
who dwells within his bhaktas' hearts,
hears them singing his praises,
he completely soaks them with bliss. 8

Those who are bound by Hari
leave everything else and abide in his constant joy,
always singing his praises.
They become full of perfect
truth, consciousness, and bliss. 9

अहं निरुद्धो रोधेन निरोधपदवीं गतः ।
निरुद्धानां तु रोधाय निरोधं वर्णयामि ते ॥१०॥

ahaṃ niruddho rodhena nirodhapadavīṃ gataḥ
10 *niruddhānāṃ tu rodhāya nirodhaṃ varṇayāmi te*

हरिणा ये विनिर्मुक्तास् ते मग्ना भवसागरे ।
ये निरुद्धास्त एवात्र मोदमायान्त्यहर्निशम् ॥११॥

hariṇā ye vinirmuktās te magnā bhavasāgare
11 *ye niruddhāsta evātra modamāyāntyaharniśam*

संसारावेश-दुष्टानाम् इन्द्रियाणां हिताय वै ।
कृष्णस्य सर्ववस्तूनि भूम्न ईशस्य योजयेत् ॥१२॥

saṃsārāveśa-duṣṭānām indriyāṇāṃ hitāya vai
12 *kṛṣṇasya sarvavastūni bhūmna īśasya yojayet*

गुणेष्वाविष्ट-चित्तानां सर्वदा मुरवैरिणः ।
संसार-विरह-क्लेशौ न स्यातां हरिवत् सुखम् ॥१३॥

guṇeṣvāviṣṭa-cittānāṃ sarvadā muravairiṇaḥ
13 *saṃsāra-viraha-kleśau na syātāṃ harivat sukham*

तदा भवेद् दयालुत्वम् अन्यथा क्रूरता मता ।
बाधशङ्काऽपि नास्त्यत्र तद् अध्यासोऽपि सिध्यति ॥१४॥

tadā bhaved dayālutvam anyathā krūratā matā
14 *bādhaśaṅkā'pi nāstyatra tad adhyāso'pi sidhyati*

I am possessed by Krishna.
I have attained this divine state of nirodha
by falling under his control.
Now I will explain the nature of nirodha
for those who are ready to be bound by Hari,
for the sake of their nirodha. 10

Those whom Hari has liberated from himself
are absorbed into the worldly ocean,
while those whom he binds to himself
surely experience supreme joy day and night. 11

For the improvement of corrupt senses
that are obsessed with the mundane world,
everything in life should be united with Shri Krishna,
the omnipresent inner-controller. 12

The blessed ones whose minds are always
filled with the divine virtues of Shri Krishna
have no worldly woes or separations.
The joy they experience is similar to Hari's. 13

For those blessed ones, Hari becomes merciful.
Otherwise, he would be perceived as heartless.
Obstructions are impossible in the devotional position,
because Shri Krishna's presence perfects everything. 14

भगवद् धर्म-सामर्थ्याद् विरागो विषये स्थिरः ।
गुणैर् हरि-सुख-स्पर्शान् न दुःखं भाति कर्हिचित् ॥ १५॥

bhagavad dharma-sāmarthyād virāgo viṣaye sthiraḥ
15 *guṇair hari-sukha-sparśān na duḥkhaṃ bhāti karhicit*

एवं ज्ञात्वा ज्ञानमार्गाद् उत्कर्षो गुणवर्णने ।
अमत्सरैर् अलुब्धैश्च वर्णनीयाः सदा गुणाः ॥ १६॥

evaṃ jñātvā jñānamārgād utkarṣo guṇavarṇane
16 *amatsarair alubdhaiśca varṇanīyāḥ sadā guṇāḥ*

हरिमूर्तिः सदा ध्येया सङ्कल्पादपि तत्र हि ।
दर्शनं स्पर्शनं स्पष्टं तथा कृति-गती सदा ॥ १७॥

harimūrtiḥ sadā dhyeyā saṅkalpādapi tatra hi
17 *darśanaṃ sparśanaṃ spaṣṭaṃ tathā kṛti-gatī sadā*

श्रवणं कीर्तनं स्पष्टं पुत्रे कृष्णप्रिये रतिः ।
पायोर् मलांश-त्यागेन शेषभागं तनौ नयेत् ॥ १८॥

śravaṇaṃ kīrtanaṃ spaṣṭaṃ putre kṛṣṇapriye ratiḥ
18 *pāyor malāṃśa-tyāgena śeṣabhāgaṃ tanau nayet*

यस्य वा भगवत्कार्यं यदा स्पष्टं न दृश्यते ।
तदा विनिग्रहस् तस्य कर्तव्य इति निश्चयः ॥ १९॥

yasya vā bhagavatkāryaṃ yadā spaṣṭaṃ na dṛśyate
19 *tadā vinigrahas tasya kartavya iti niścayaḥ*

The power of the Beloved's divine virtues
creates firm distaste for worldliness.
If Shri Krishna's blissful essence
is touched while singing his glories,
one will never experience mundane suffering again. 15

Singing about beloved Hari
is superior to the path of knowledge.
And so, free of jealousy and greed,
bhaktas should always praise his divine virtues. 16

Always reflect on Hari's form with conviction.
See and touch him clearly.
Make every movement always for him. 17

Sing and listen to his glories carefully.
Have loving exchanges with your spouse
to have a child who is beloved to Shri Krishna.
Even the passing of stool is so that the body
will be refreshed and useful in his seva. 18

If you recognize that your actions
are not clearly connected to the blessed Lord,
then you should without a doubt control them. 19

नातः परतरो मन्त्रो नातः परतरः स्तवः ।
नातः परतरा विद्या तीर्थं नातः परात्परम् ॥२०॥

nātaḥ paratarо mantro nātaḥ parataraḥ stavaḥ
20 *nātaḥ paratarā vidyā tīrthaṃ nātaḥ parātparam*

॥इति श्रीवल्लभाचार्य-विरचितम् निरोधलक्षणम् सम्पूर्णम् ॥
iti śrīvallabhācārya-viracitam nirodhalakṣaṇam sampūrṇam

There is no mantra,
prayer, knowledge, or holy place
superior to this blessed state of nirodha. 20

Thus ends Nirodha Lakṣaṇam by Shri Vallabhacharya.

सेवाफलम् स-विवरणम्

Sevā Phalam Sa-Vivaraṇam

The Rewards of Seva

The last of the *16 Works* was taught by Shri Vallabhacharya to Vishnudas in 1526 CE. Since Vishnudas had difficulty understanding the instructions given in this text, Shri Vallabhacharya composed his own commentary, called *Vivaraṇam*, which has also been partially incorporated into this translation. The master speaks of both the three-fold rewards and hindrances that can arise in seva. Anxiety should be abandoned in all circumstances, because the giving of the divine reward is in God's hands.

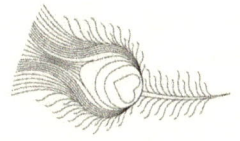

यादृशी सेवना प्रोक्ता तत्सिद्धौ फलमुच्यते।
अलौकिकस्य दाने हि चाद्यः सिध्येन् मनोरथः ॥ १॥
फलं वा ह्यधिकारो वा न कालोऽत्र नियामकम्।

yādṛśī sevanā proktā tatsiddhau phalamucyate
1 *alaukikasya dāne hi cādyaḥ sidhyen manorathaḥ*
2a *phalaṃ vā hyadhikāro vā na kālo'tra niyāmakam*

॥विवरणम् ॥
सेवायां फलत्रयम् अलौकिक-सामर्थ्यं
सायुज्यं सेवोपयोगिदेहो वैकुण्ठादिषु

Vivaraṇam: *sevāyāṁ phalatrayam alaukika-sāmarthyaṁ sāyujyaṁ sevopayogideho vaikuṇṭhādiṣu*

उद्वेगः प्रतिबन्धो वा भोगो वा स्यात्तु बाधकम् ॥ २॥

2b *udvegaḥ pratibandho vā bhogo vā syāttu bādhakaṃ*

॥विवरणम् ॥
सेवायां प्रतिबन्धक-त्रयम् उद्वेगः प्रतिबन्धो भोगो वा।
त्रयाणां साधनपरित्यागः कर्तव्यः।

Vivaraṇam: *sevāyāṁ pratibandhaka-trayam udvegaḥ pratibandho bhogo vā. trayāṇāṁ sādhanaparityāgaḥ kartavyaḥ.*

अकर्तव्यं भगवतः सर्वथा चेद् गतिर् न हि।
यथा वा तत्त्व-निर्धारो विवेकः साधनं मतम् ॥ ३॥

akartavyaṃ bhagavataḥ sarvathā ced gatir na hi
3 *yathā vā tattva-nirdhāro vivekaḥ sādhanaṃ matam*

As I have explained before
in the *Pearl Necklace Teachings*,
true seva arises when the mind and heart
are threaded into the blessed practice
of worshipping Shri Krishna.
Now I will explain the rewards of this seva
when it is perfectly performed.

From the moment the blessed Lord
gives the divine reward of his presence,
the bhakta's spiritual desires are fulfilled. 1

Time is never a controlling factor
regarding eligibility and the three rewards of seva:
to experience transcendent love (*alaukika-sāmarthya*),
to be absorbed into God's lila (*sāyujya*),
and to attain a spiritual form (*sevopayogideha*)
useful in eternal realms. 2a

Anxiety (*udvega*),
obstructions (*pratibandha*),
and worldly enjoyment (*bhoga*)
are the three hindrances to seva. 2b

If for any reason the blessed Lord
does not desire to give a reward,
then there is simply no solution.
In that case, the practitioner's approach
is to wisely assess the truth of the situation. 3

बाधकानां परित्यागो भोगेप्येकं तथा परम् ।
निष्प्रत्यूहं महान् भोगः प्रथमे विशते सदा ॥४॥

bādhakānāṃ parityāgo bhogepyekaṃ tathā param
4 *niṣpratyūhaṃ mahān bhogaḥ prathame viśate sadā*

॥विवरणम् ॥

भोगो द्विविधः लौकिकोऽलौकिकश्च । तत्र लौकिकस् त्याज्य एव । अलौकिकस्तु फलानां मध्ये प्रथमे प्रविशति । प्रतिबन्धोऽपि द्विविधः साधारणो भगवत्कृतश्च । तत्र आद्यो बुद्ध्या त्याज्यः । भगवत्कृतश्चेत् प्रतिबन्धः तदा भगवान् फलं न दास्यतीति मन्तव्यम् । तदा अन्यसेवापि व्यर्था । तदा आसुरोऽयं जीव इति निर्धारः । तदा ज्ञानमार्गेण स्थातव्यं शोकाभावायेति विवेकः । ननु साधारणो भोगः कथं त्यक्तव्य इत्याकांक्षायामाह सविघ्नोऽल्पो घातकः स्याद् इति ।

Vivaraṇam: *bhogo dvividhaḥ laukiko'laukikaśca. tatra laukikas-tyājya eva. alaukikastu phalānāṁ madhye prathame praviśati. pratibandho'pi dvividhaḥ sādhāraṇo bhagavatkṛtaśca. tatra ādyo buddhyā tyājyaḥ. bhagavatkṛtaścet pratibandhaḥ tadā bhagavān phalaṁ na dāsyatīti mantavyam. tadā anyasevāpi vyarthā. tadā āsuro'yaṁ jīva iti nirdhāraḥ. tadā jñānamārgeṇa sthātavyaṁ śokābhāvāyeti vivekaḥ. nanu sādhāraṇo bhogaḥ kathaṁ tyaktavya ityākāṁkṣāyāmāha savighno'lpo ghātakaḥ syād iti.*

There is a divine enjoyment,
the Krishna reward,
which is free from every impediment.

Worldly enjoyment
and the other hindrances I mentioned
should be totally abandoned,
but know that both
God-created hindrances and divine rewards
are always beyond the bhakta's control. 4

सविघ्नोऽल्पो घातकः स्याद् बलाद्-एतौ सदा मतौ।

5a *savighno'lpo ghātakaḥ syād balād-etau sadā matau*

॥विवरणम्॥

सविघ्नत्वाद् अल्पत्वाद् भोगस्त्याज्यः एतौ प्रतिबन्धकौ।

Vivaraṇam: *savighnatvād alpatvād bhogastyājyaḥ etau pratibandhakau.*

द्वितीये सर्वथा चिन्ता त्याज्या संसारनिश्चयात्॥५॥

5b *dvitīye sarvathā cintā tyājyā saṃsāraniścayāt*

॥विवरणम्॥

द्वितीयो भगवत्कृतप्रतिबन्धः।

ज्ञानस्थित्यभावे चिन्ताभावार्थमाह द्वितीय इति

Vivaraṇam: *dvitīyo bhagavatkṛtapratibandhaḥ. jñānasthityabhāve cintābhāvārthamāha dvitīya iti*

न त्वाद्ये दातृता नास्ति तृतीये बाधकं गृहम्।

6a *na tvādye dātṛtā nāsti tṛtīye bādhakaṃ gṛham*

॥विवरणम्॥

आद्यफलाभावे भगवतो दातृत्वं नास्ति। तदा सेवा नाधिदैविकी इत्युक्तं भवति। भोगाभावस् तदैव सिध्यति यदा गृह-परित्यागः।

Vivaraṇam: *ādyaphalābhāve bhagavato dātṛtvaṁ nāsti. tadā sevā nādhidaivikī ityuktaṁ bhavati. bhogābhāvas tadaiva sidhyati yadā gṛha-parityāgaḥ.*

Worldly enjoyment
is insignificant and destructive.
One should always consider
these two aspects of
worldly enjoyment to be powerful. 5a

One should also renounce anxiety
concerning any God-created obstruction;
it should be seen simply as
a movement within mundane reality. 5b

If anxiety, the first hindrance, arises,
it should be understood that the blessed Lord
is simply not ready to give a reward at that time.

In the third hindrance, worldly enjoyment,
the mundane home is the obstacle.

Always consider these hindrances to be
beyond the bhakta's jurisdiction. 6a

अवश्येयं सदा भाव्या सर्वम् अन्यन् मनोभ्रमः ॥६॥

6b *avaśyeyaṃ sadā bhāvyā sarvam anyan manobhramaḥ*

तदीयैरपि तत् कार्यं पुष्टौ नैव विलम्बयेत् ।
गुणक्षोभेऽपि द्रष्टव्यम् एतदेवेति मे मतिः ॥७॥

tadīyairapi tat kāryaṃ puṣṭau naiva vilambayet
7 *guṇakṣobhe'pi draṣṭavyam etadeveti me matiḥ*

कुसृष्टिर् अत्र वा काचिद् उत्पद्येत स वै भ्रमः ॥८॥

8 *kusṛṣṭir atra vā kācid utpadyeta sa vai bhramaḥ*

॥ इति श्रीवल्लभाचार्य-विरचितं स-विवरणम् सेवा-फलं सम्पूर्णम् ॥

iti śrīvallabhācārya-viracitaṃ
sa-vivaraṇam sevā-phalaṃ sampūrṇam

Any other thought on the subject
is mere confusion. 6b

Those bhaktas who belong to Krishna
should consider these teachings
concerning rewards and hindrances
and know that Shri Krishna
does not delay the rewarding of his grace.

Even if you are afflicted
by the movements of the material world,
recognize the truths
that I have established in this teaching.
This is my opinion. 7

Any distortion that might arise here
is mere delusion. 8

Thus ends Sevā Phalam with Vivaraṇam commentary,
composed by Shri Vallabhacharya.

श्रीमधुराष्टकम्

Śrī Madhurāṣṭakam

The Song of Sweetness

In this famous composition in praise of Shri Krishna's sweetness, Shri Vallabhacharya remembers his beloved Shri Krishna, his lips, his face, and everything connected to him. Numerous loving lilas are also hidden within the master's lines. These verses are sung throughout India.

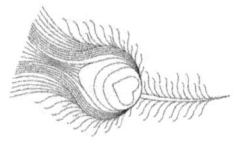

अधरं मधुरं वदनं मधुरं नयनं मधुरं हसितं मधुरम्।
हृदयं मधुरं गमनं मधुरं मधुराधिपतेर् अखिलं मधुरम्॥१॥

adharaṃ *madhuraṃ* **vadanaṃ** *madhuraṃ*
nayanaṃ *madhuraṃ* **hasitaṃ** *madhuram*
hṛdayaṃ *madhuraṃ* **gamanaṃ** *madhuraṃ*
1 *madhurādhipater akhilaṃ madhuram*

वचनं मधुरं चरितं मधुरं वसनं मधुरं वलितं मधुरम्।
चलितं मधुरं भ्रमितं मधुरं मधुराधिपतेर् अखिलं मधुरम्॥२॥

vacanaṃ *madhuraṃ* **caritaṃ** *madhuraṃ*
vasanaṃ *madhuraṃ* **valitaṃ** *madhuram*
calitaṃ *madhuraṃ* **bhramitaṃ** *madhuraṃ*
2 *madhurādhipater akhilaṃ madhuram*

वेणुर्मधुरो रेणुर्मधुरः पाणिर्मधुरः पादौ मधुरौ।
नृत्यं मधुरं सख्यं मधुरं मधुराधिपतेर् अखिलं मधुरम्॥३॥

veṇur *madhuro* **reṇur** *madhuraḥ*
pāṇir *madhuraḥ* **pādau** *madhurau*
nṛtyaṃ *madhuraṃ* **sakhyaṃ** *madhuraṃ*
3 *madhurādhipater akhilaṃ madhuram*

गीतं मधुरं पीतं मधुरं भुक्तं मधुरं सुप्तं मधुरम्।
रूपं मधुरं तिलकं मधुरं मधुराधिपतेर् अखिलं मधुरम्॥४॥

gītaṃ *madhuraṃ* **pītaṃ** *madhuraṃ*
bhuktaṃ *madhuraṃ* **suptaṃ** *madhuram*
rūpaṃ *madhuraṃ* **tilakaṃ** *madhuraṃ*
4 *madhurādhipater akhilaṃ madhuram*

His lips are sweet. His face is sweet.
His eyes are sweet. His laugh is sweet.
His heart is sweet. His movement is sweet.
Shri Krishna is the Lord of sweetness and
everything is sweet. 1

His speech is sweet. His character is sweet.
His cloth is sweet. His fatigue is sweet.
His walk is sweet. His meanderings are sweet.
Shri Krishna is the Lord of sweetness and
everything is sweet. 2

His flute is sweet. The sands are sweet.
His hands are sweet. His feet are sweet.
His dance is sweet. His friendship is sweet.
Shri Krishna is the Lord of sweetness and
everything is sweet. 3

His song is sweet. His yellow shawl is sweet.
His enjoyment is sweet. His sleep is sweet.
His form is sweet. His tilak (forehead adornment) is sweet.
Shri Krishna is the Lord of sweetness and
everything is sweet. 4

करणं मधुरं तरणं मधुरं हरणं मधुरं रमणं मधुरम् ।
वमितं मधुरं शमितं मधुरं मधुराधिपतेर् अखिलं मधुरम् ॥ ५॥

karaṇaṃ *madhuraṃ* **taraṇaṃ** *madhuraṃ*
haraṇaṃ *madhuraṃ* **ramaṇaṃ** *madhuram*
vamitaṃ *madhuraṃ* **śamitaṃ** *madhuraṃ*
5 *madhurādhipater akhilaṃ madhuram*

गुञ्जा मधुरा माला मधुरा यमुना मधुरा विची मधुरा ।
सलिलं मधुरं कमलं मधुरं मधुराधिपतेर् अखिलं मधुरम् ॥ ६॥

guñjā *madhurā* **mālā** *madhurā*
yamunā *madhurā* **vicī** *madhurā*
salilaṃ *madhuraṃ* **kamalaṃ** *madhuraṃ*
6 *madhurādhipater akhilaṃ madhuram*

गोपी मधुरा लीला मधुरा युक्तं मधुरं मुक्तं मधुरम् ।
इष्टं मधुरं शिष्टं मधुरं मधुराधिपतेर् अखिलं मधुरम् ॥ ७॥

gopī *madhurā* **līlā** *madhurā*
yuktaṃ *madhuraṃ* **muktaṃ** *madhuram*
iṣṭaṃ *madhuraṃ* **śiṣṭaṃ** *madhuraṃ*
7 *madhurādhipater akhilaṃ madhuram*

गोपा मधुरा गावो मधुरा यष्टिर्मधुरा सृष्टिर्मधुरा ।
दलितं मधुरं फलितं मधुरं मधुराधिपतेर् अखिलं मधुरम् ॥ ८॥

gopā *madhurā* **gāvo** *madhurā*
yaṣṭir *madhurā* **sṛṣṭir** *madhurā*
dalitaṃ *madhuraṃ* **phalitaṃ** *madhuraṃ*
8 *madhurādhipater akhilaṃ madhuram*

॥इति श्रीवल्लभाचार्य-विरचितं श्रीमधुराष्टकम् सम्पूर्णम् ॥
iti śrīvallabhācārya-viracitaṃ śrīmadhurāṣṭakam sampūrṇam

His doings are sweet. His crossing is sweet.
His stealing is sweet. His dalliance is sweet.
His chewed betel is sweet. His tranquility is sweet.
Shri Krishna is the Lord of sweetness and
everything is sweet. 5

His gunja beads are sweet. His necklaces are sweet.
The Yamuna River is sweet. The waves are sweet.
The water is sweet. The lotus is sweet.
Shri Krishna is the Lord of sweetness and
everything is sweet. 6

The gopis are sweet. The lila is sweet.
The union is sweet. Liberation is sweet.
Desire is sweet. His control is sweet.
Shri Krishna is the Lord of sweetness and
everything is sweet. 7

The cowlads are sweet. The cows are sweet.
His cane is sweet. Creation is sweet.
Destruction is sweet. The fruit is sweet.
Shri Krishna is the Lord of sweetness and
everything is sweet. 8

Thus ends Śrī Madhurāṣṭakam by Shri Vallabhacharya.

शिक्षापद्यानि

Śikṣā Padyāni

The Last Teachings

Shri Vallabhacharya left his home to spend his last days by the banks of the Ganga River at Hanuman Ghat in Benares. His two sons and several close followers went there to receive the last teachings. Just before the silent master entered the Ganga and merged with his body into a column of light to ascend to his Beloved, he wrote three-and-a-half lines of devotional counsel in the sands.

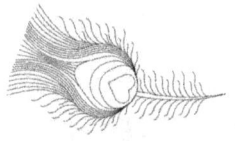

यदा बहिर्मुखाः यूयं भविष्यथ कथञ्चन।
तदा कालप्रवाहस्था देहचित्तादयोऽप्युत ॥१॥

yadā bahirmukhāḥ yūyaṃ bhaviṣyatha kathañcana
1 *tadā kālapravāhasthā dehacittādayo'pyuta*

सर्वथा भक्षयिष्यन्ति युष्मान् इति मतिर् मम।
न लौकिकः प्रभुः कृष्णो मनुते नैव लौकिकम् ॥२॥

sarvathā bhakṣayiṣyanti yuṣmān iti matir mama
2 *na laukikaḥ prabhuḥ kṛṣṇo manute naiva laukikam*

भावस् तत्राऽप्यस्मदीयः सर्वस्वश्चैहिकश्च सः।
परलोकश्च तेनायं सर्वभावेन सर्वथा ॥३॥

bhāvas tatrā'pyasmadīyaḥ sarvasvaścaihikaśca saḥ
3 *paralokaśca tenāyaṃ sarvabhāvena sarvathā*

सेव्यः स एव गोपीशो विधास्यत्यखिलं हि नः ॥४॥

4 *sevyaḥ sa eva gopīśo vidhāsyatyakhilaṃ hi naḥ*

मयि चेद् अस्ति विश्वासः श्रीगोपीजनवल्लभे।
तदा कृतार्था यूयं हि शोचनीयं न कर्हिचित् ॥
मुक्तिर् हित्वाऽन्यथ-रूपं स्वरूपेण व्यवस्थितिः ॥

mayi ced asti viśvāsaḥ śrīgopījanavallabhe
tadā kṛtārthā yūyaṃ hi śocanīyaṃ na karhicit
muktir hitvā'nyatha-rūpaṃ svarūpeṇa vyavasthitiḥ

If you ever turn away from Shri Krishna,
your body and mind,
along with everything that exists
within the flow of time, 1
will always be devoured.
This is my belief.

Shri Krishna is not mundane,
nor does he accept
the worship of worldly people. 2

Our bhava for him,
in this world or in any other,
is our all and everything. 3

The Lord of the gopis is to be worshipped
with every devotional feeling,
at all times. 4

[Shri Krishna then appeared and gave this final teaching:]

If you believe in me,
the beloved of the gopis,
you are spiritually accomplished,
and there is absolutely
nothing else to be concerned with.

After leaving everything worldly,
you then become established
in the form of liberation.

Lover's Life

Lover's Life arises from teachings originally presented by Shrimad Vallabhacharya in his Sanskrit teaching *Viveka Dhairyāśrayaḥ* (*Wisdom, Perseverance, and Refuge*) as well as the later Sanskrit commentaries on that work. It is a practical guide filled with wise advice on how to live in the world, deal with obstructions, and maintain a rich devotional life. It also speaks of, in a discreet way, the higher devotional states that flourish between the beloved and his loved ones. Unity between the non-material, perfect lila realm and this world of changes is skillfully navigated by the bhakta, who is wise enough to fathom her life as part of the beloved's love games and strong enough to weather all karmic afflictions and stand firmly situated in his sanctuary. This is Shri Vallabhacharya's essential message.

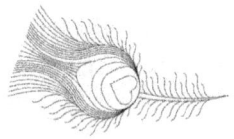

The blessed soul becomes engaged to the beloved when there is a heartfelt acceptance of bhakti, an entrance into the path of love. Then she will do anything for him. She becomes the beloved's divine lover and is committed to his *seva*—his service and pleasure. This is a selfless spiritual art. When the beloved's delights are sought, there is transformation and victory over the small self. Then the yogic love can be reciprocated. This is devotion. It is known to the bhakta, the follower and lover of God.

Shri Mahaprabhu Vallabhacharya has mentioned in his *Navaratna* (*Nine Jewels*) that the bhakta must leave all forms of anxiety before the beloved can be pleased. When the mind and heart are infested with worldly woes, his delights cannot be appropriately considered. Wisdom arises when hindering concerns are dropped and there is dedication to his seva, his pleasing service. For this, three bhakti ingredients are essential. The lover of Hari must possess wisdom and the ability to set her priorities correctly. She must also stand strong in her world and remain unmoved by negative forces. Finally, her refuge in the beloved, her blessed Hari, must be willful and firm. Shri Mahaprabhuji begins his teaching with a devotional definition of wisdom:

Always protect your discrimination and perseverance,
and carefully nourish divine refuge.
True wisdom is seeing that beloved Hari
1 *will accomplish everything according to his own will.*

The key to wisdom and fortitude is refuge in the beloved. When she remains in his haven, knowledge and strength flourish under his loving protection. Beloved Hari, the perfect one, is also the purifier who eradicates the sins and sorrows of his lovers. To grasp this is knowledge.

To rely merely on the merit of one's own strength can bring forth pride and a false sense of accomplishment, which is not pleasing to the beloved. Wisdom is knowing without a doubt that, "My beloved will take care of me."

Anxiety plagues the bhakta-lover when she temporarily forgets his loving embrace. When her wisdom returns, she knows she is protected. All is seen as perfect and part of the beloved's process, a portion of his faultless lila. When the lover rests in his glow, his sweet will can be seen. Then, without asking, everything is accomplished.

The lover first identifies the beloved's lila, his perfect play, and then finds his company. Finally, she embraces the beloved's delectable resolve. She feels it in every circumstance and while surrendering to his notions, she is purified. She desires to touch him, and when Hari recognizes her intention, the beloved falls for her.

In that loving congregation, what need could there be to pray for anything besides his association? Why trouble the beloved when he is going to give more than what can be asked for? This is the bhakta-lover's view, her subtle law of insight. Wisdom is knowing his perfect power and seeing that his decisions are lila-precise. Hari's will is what makes things happen, not happen, as well as what is beyond the two.

With insight, the lover rests firmly in his haven, never wandering from his embrace. Whatever is essential for the lover and her development is always given without asking. In the Hari romance, the beloved practice, even the attainment of liberation pales in comparison to what is freely given.

What is the use of prayer?
Why request something from him?
This only happens when there is a doubt
in the intention of his perfect plan.
Hari is everywhere, and he is everything.
2 *He is compelling and potent.*

Why ask, when it is already given? Why hanker, when the greatest riches are at hand? A prayer for something arises from a doubt that it will not arise. Prayer for this or for that comes from forgetfulness. It occurs when the lover overlooks the fact that everything has already been taken care of.

What is given is good; what is not given is also fine. Although it is sometimes hard to discern at the time of encounter, life for the lover is always perfect. For her, gain and loss are always absolutely accurate.

What is truly needed is given, directly or indirectly. The lover never thinks, "I can get it myself." Such a person is like a dwarf in a ditch who reaches for a lofty fruit. He tires from the stretch and does not understand that the reward will cascade down to him at just the right time.

The beloved will never supply what is detrimental to his bhakta-lover. He knows, for he is in all places, there at all times. The beloved manifests everywhere and even becomes all things. Even knowing some of this removes all doubts regarding his intentions. The bhakta sees the beloved's accomplishments everywhere. This is not a passive acceptance of life. Knowing the beloved's will is dynamic, transforming, and compelling for the bhakta. It is her perfect part in the play of total love, the beloved practice.

To turn from the love games to the small self or to try to manipulate situations with exertion and pride-filled practices is a fall from love, a slip from his embrace. The small-self view is always narrow and ineffective. Moreover, it is plagued with fear and false expectations of agreeable results. It lacks Hari's essential refuge and clings to the impermanent nature of things. Wisdom is to graciously accept whatever the beloved gives and to feel Hari's acceptance in every situation. Wisdom is to avoid all forms of spiritual arrogance.

These are some of her views of *seva*, the pleasing worship of the beloved with one's mind, body, and wealth. It arises naturally with unconditional refuge. It connects at the source and illuminates all portions of life. Just as dirty water that enters the Ganges River becomes Ganga and is worshipped as such, in the state of refuge, false identification is sundered. It merges with the higher self, and then everything becomes perfect, like Ganga. Everything is the beloved's. She is the beloved's, and then the beloved becomes hers. When Hari envelops everything, there is a transformation.

Leave completely all sense of false pride
and cherish the feeling of being under Hari's rule.
Then, when there is a special command,
the beloved enters the heart. 3
In that extraordinary circumstance,
the bhava that is intuited is never worldly;
it is separate from the concerns of the physical body.

How pleasant it is to be under Hari's total control. In that blessed situation, one can never be taken advantage of. In illumination, the lover becomes spiritually adorned. The beauty of any physical body could never compare to hers. The lover of Hari skillfully maintains her unique, grace-filled style. In her continual remembrance, she remains identified with the lila form. Each sense is connected and enveloped in the samadhi of her beloved. She is under Hari's sway, and then Hari falls under hers. The romance is unending. The beloved is her lila-master, and his response is forever appropriate and exact.

In the romance, the Hari one, the *mayic* (illusory) world is forgotten. The force of Hari's love purifies the lover until everything else is simply forgotten. This love affair is not made—it emerges. When a worldly romance cannot be forced to arise, then what to say of the Hari one! You can only avail yourself, ready yourself to be enveloped by him. You can only prepare yourself by giving everything else up. Divine romance is not attained with meditative effort—it is spontaneous. It is not prolonged by any practice, but by intention.

In that blessed Hari romance, the focus falls effortlessly upon the beautiful Brahman. What follows is a total forgetfulness of *samsara*. For the true lover, renunciation never arises out of hatred, but rather from an appreciation of a higher taste. When priorities become refined, defined, and directed to the beloved, then other unrelated flavors begin to appear spiritless. What is not connected with her beloved no longer holds any interest. She wants to follow him everywhere. Her dharma, the devotional one, is to be constantly by his side. This is wisdom. This is also insight.

The lover enters the haven of the beloved with the help of *satsang*, the association of his other lovers. There is no jealousy amongst them. In the bhakti arena, the spirit of dedication is heightened by mutual reflection.

Whatever situation Hari puts his bhakta-lover into or through, whether it has to do with the connected or unconnected family, with friends, or other associates, every situation in the world occurs because of the beloved's lila. It is seen as arising because of his sporting nature. Everything else seems unreal. The bhakta-lover who understands this has an unconditional acceptance of every situation. She knows and sees that Hari has created everything. Then there is freedom, a release from all false expectations and useless concerns for the inevitable. That which does not vanish becomes consecrated.

The lover lives in her world with comprehension. Behind the worldly existence wells her ocean of devotion. Her service and loyalty are all governed from the perspective of increasing his dalliance. Now, she alone can remove his anguish.

Sometimes there is a special command, a wish that comes directly from the beloved to his bhakta. It can arrive through the guru, or it can arise in a dream or from a celestial song. It can flow from another lover, or it can be seen in the heart. At times, even the beloved can appear directly before his lover and hand it to her. This is *darshan.*

Until the lover receives the beloved's directions, she continues her practice and waits, according to the revealed teachings. Refinement is knowing how to decipher the beloved's special wishes from mundane ones. Insight is knowing how much to practice and how much to wait. When the remarkable request arises, the lover follows the divine design and uses the communication to deepen her lila entrance. She will adorn Hari accordingly, as she penetrates his special communication.

The special command should never be confused with anything worldly, which would pay disrespect to the beloved. It is in all cases distinct from the bodily situation, yet it comes through it. The special command never has anything to do with any worldly gain. It is not for the sake of marriage or money. It will never instruct the lover on how to increase worldly wealth, prestige, or desire. The special command is showered to enhance the lover's lila entrance. Knowing this important distinction between the divine and worldly order makes the lover insightful.

Devotional direction is laid out by the guru (outer and inner) and only shifted with the direct endorsement of Hari. The beloved's personal directions override all other instructions. They spring from the source and are undiluted truths.

For the calling to arise and become firm, the root practice is to cultivate the ability to rest in the beloved's refuge. Then the lover, in her quest for his shelter, takes the company of other divinely afflicted lovers who know of his union. They keep the beloved and his ways within their devotional heart. Only with his other lovers will she share her secrets. Hari works through their assembly.

The lover is content when she receives *prasada*, the beloved's grace. She lives on his leftovers and engages only in as many worldly activities as necessary to maintain a balance. Poise in all spheres is essential for the growth of devotion. For the sake of devotional stability in her romance, she renounces all sense of obstinacy regarding worldly matters. The lover can do this, for she knows that the beloved provides everything necessary. To live in this gentle harmony between all activities, worldly and divine, is a matter of wisdom and insight.

Although it is necessary to obtain wealth for one's offerings and general living, the bhakta never sets up false standards; she knows that Hari provides. She follows the beloved's will and is never inflexible.

Whatever the difficult circumstance,
never be uncompromising. 4
Without being obstinate,
maintain a keen sense of awareness in all situations,
and recognize what is dharma and what is not.
This is my explanation of wisdom.

In any difficult situation, such as a change in lifestyle that occurs because of events beyond the lover's control or because of wealth or misfortune, the bhakta never forces the circumstances. She makes the necessary adjustments. While being flexible, she remembers that it is all part of her beloved's lila. Hari, the lila director, creates all parts, and his lover appreciates every role.

In the case of financial loss, if the opulence of the loving worship needs to be adjusted, the bhakta does so, always without obstinacy. If she gathers great riches, she will never falsely identify with them, for she knows that the authentic affluence is wisdom experienced in the wealth of bhava. Her spiritual value lies in how deeply her devotion is felt for Hari. In the Hari relationship, the beloved graciously accepts the lover's bhava and is never moved by other riches. The lover goes on maintaining that secret relationship and also moves responsibly through the world. In every circumstance, her Hari bhava is constant. She is sensitive to the necessary adjustments and never loses sight of her beloved. Her state is one of wisdom; she is filled with insight.

The loving relationship, the Hari romance and seva, is the lover's priority. When other social and religious obligations arise, she attends to them only when she can slip away from the beloved without disturbing his worship. The beloved's necessities are paramount for her. At the same time, she is also careful not to agitate any worldly situation. She skillfully attends social events without letting anything upset her Hari bhava on her climb to his chambers.

Once there, she becomes totally enveloped in his loving illumination. Her addiction to him no longer allows for other activities. Until that state of Hari addiction is reached, a flexible balance of action and inaction is adopted by the lover. In this regard, she always maintains a keen awareness of what is righteous and what is not. She lives in the spirit of devotion, within a dharma where exalted enthusiasm, bhava for her beloved, reigns at all times and places.

For the lover, dharma is not merely righteousness, but the ability to have bhava for Hari at all times, in every circumstance. If impurity arises due to either an action or inaction, or if there is a loss of dharma, the lover in her own brilliant way makes the necessary adjustments. In so doing, the secret relationship flourishes. She remembers the divine order of things and then acts accordingly. In all circumstances, she puts her beloved first and then arranges her worldly and religious calendar. With him first, there can never be fault or loss.

Bhagavat dharma, the dharma of Hari, is compelling

and replete. When attention is fixed on dharma, there is always accomplishment everywhere. The lover knows that to be obstinate in either the performance or non-performance of other duties creates imbalance. She knows that equilibrium is necessary in lives that are simultaneously divine, spiritual, and worldly. To be insightful in all circumstances, while maintaining harmony, is wisdom.

If the lover is blessed with a decree from the beloved, in that special circumstance, she remains sensitive to his longings and directions. Sensitivity to the beloved's agenda requires constant perseverance. Even in times of stress, when the lover may become concerned, she understands that, in Shri Mahaprabhuji's words, "Hari is going to do whatever he wants, according to his play, so stop worrying immediately."

To remain in the blessed state of remembrance, every situation must be endured, assimilated, and transformed into a lila occurrence.

Now I will speak of perseverance. 5
Perseverance is to always endure the three types of pain
(mundane, spiritual, and divine) until death.
To accomplish this, understand the body
to be like buttermilk, which remains unaffected
even after it has been beaten and robbed of its butter.
Also comprehend the spiritual pains of King Bharat,
who underwent three births before he became enlightened,
as well as the divine pangs of separation from Shri Krishna
that the gopis of Vrindavan experienced. 6

The lover endures every hardship for the beloved. Worldly affliction comes from the body; spiritual adversity arises from the senses, while divine distress surges from the depths of the soul.

Sometimes there is suffering because of an examination, a test of the lover's fortitude, to make her stronger. At other times, pain may come from past karmas. There is also divine suffering, a special award. It can occur because of the lover's unfulfilled desire to be with the beloved. It can also happen because she desires to present him with something beyond her reach. These are lila trials and surge from the love-filled heart towards Hari.

Whenever any of these threefold afflictions occurs, a disturbance can arise in either the body, senses, or soul. If not contained, they can become detrimental to the lover's *seva*—her divine pleasing service, the beloved practice. In circumstances when the lover endures, living for the sake of her beloved, she prevails.

See worldly pain in the example of buttermilk. In India, buttermilk is made from yogurt. Water is added to yogurt and then it is churned until the butter separates from the watery mixture. After the butter is removed, what is left is called buttermilk. It is considered to be without essence—that is, without butter.

As buttermilk does not feel any pain or loss of pride after the butter is removed, similarly, the lover never feels any deficit from worldly situations, regardless of how she is churned. She maintains this balanced view in loss or gain, whether it concerns wealth, wife, children, friends, or other associates. If worldly agitations create a gulf and distance from the beloved, the lover remembers how the buttermilk was churned and then, without any sense of ownership, she abandons the butter and never thinks of it again.

If the lover is ever insulted, treated unfairly, or finds herself in any negative situation arising from contact with *samsara*, the *mayic* creation, she reflects upon buttermilk. The buttermilk was beaten and robbed of its essence, yet it felt no pain or loss. The buttermilk was happy to be fat-free.

The only butter the lover requires is unconditional love. It is the true substance and cannot be stolen. Once tasted, it makes everything else seem unrelated. She finds nourishment in exalted relations with other Hari lovers. Blessed associations enhance her relationship with the beloved. These satsangs are found in this world but are not worldly. She recognizes them and welcomes their nectars of devotion. They are cherished.

Affliction can also arise from the senses. When the senses are agitated, or when they hanker after something without understanding the nature of impermanence, the result is suffering. The senses become disturbed by anger and jealousy. To deal with discursive senses that are disregarding the beloved, the story of King Bharat should be remembered. He never forgot his Hari bhava throughout his difficult and unusual journey.

Bharat was a great Indian king who lived long ago. India, also called Bharat, was named after him. After ruling for many years, he renounced his kingdom and retired to the forest for enlightenment practices.

One day while Bharat was meditating by a riverbank, a pregnant deer being pursued by a tiger jumped into the river. The deer died in the leap, but not before giving birth to a fawn. The king took the newborn fawn into his care and soon became excessively attached to it. Shortly thereafter, the king died. Since he was constantly thinking about the fawn, and the subject of one's mind at the time of death determines one's next incarnation, the king was reborn as a deer, with complete memory of his previous birth. As a deer, he stayed near a sage's ashram. He ate the sage's leftovers and focused his mind on the highest pursuit of life. Soon he dropped that form and was born again, this time as a Brahmin man.

Not wanting to be obstructed in his path by anyone or thing, the Brahmin behaved in front of others like a mad fool. After his father died, he wandered the world. Once when he was captured to be used as a human sacrifice, he remained totally fearless. When the appointed hour arrived, a goddess manifested in the sacrificial hall and saved him by killing all of his captors.

Bharat's wandering continued, until one day a king who was in search of enlightenment happened upon him. This king needed an extra bearer to carry his palanquin. Bharat, now appearing as the Brahmin fool, agreed to carry the king's palanquin, but when he didn't keep pace with the other bearers, the king reprimanded him. When Bharat replied that his stride was unique, the king realized that the great enlightenment teacher he had been seeking was there below him. He climbed down from his palanquin and became Bharat's humble disciple.

It was only after many trials that King Bharat attained his goal of God realization. Regardless of his wandering senses, he persevered and kept his focus. Similarly, the lover who remains firmly established in devotion, regardless of the worldly situation, becomes a vessel for bhava. With Hari's remembrance, there are no obstructions. In that blessed state, the song continues.

Divine pain, the anguish of the devotional heart,

arises from direct connection to the beloved. He sports with his lovers in a lila hide-and-seek. Sometimes he may delay, but when the fruit is finally given, it is totally sweet and worth the wait. Only love can influence the beloved. Still, the lover who desires to be taken into the beloved's arms uses every resource to find him. She waits, practices, cries and contemplates, yet the beloved may still not appear.

The greatest example of this fire-like devotion is found in the bhakti of the svaminis of Vrindavan, the gopis of Braja. Once when Krishna went to the forest and sounded his sweet flute, its enchanting call brought those accomplished souls, the dairymaids of Braja, out of their worldly homes into his presence. Meanwhile, some gopis were caught in their homes, unable to leave. They were stopped by their husbands and other family members and could not join the others in the Krishna congregation deep within the groves of Vrindavan.

Those gopis who remained stuck in their homes did not view Krishna as the divine beloved, but rather saw him as their worldly paramour. This material view is what really kept them ensnared in their homes. Their desires for the beloved had specific motives and were tainted with worldly stuff that restricted their movements in bhakti. The delay in their Krishna meeting afflicted their souls. They knew they were missing the beloved's dance, his *Rasa Lila*, a congregation of elixirs.

Unable to find their way out of their worldly homes, those gopis closed their eyes and meditated upon the form of their beloved. At that moment, they experienced his intense pangs of separation. In a single second, an affliction equal to countless years in hell filled their beings.

That fire of separation swept through their karmic lots and cleansed them of all previous obstructions.

Then, within their meditation, the blessed form of Hari emerged and embraced them. From his touch, a joy arose that was equal to the concentrated pleasure of a billion years in heaven. In the intensity of the experience, those blessed lovers left their material forms and joined their beloved in the eternal abode. They had become partners in the love games.

The gopis who did make it out of their homes reached the forests of Vrindavan, only to be told by Shri Krishna to return home to their worldly lives. They did not listen to his words, for they knew that they were laced with double meanings. His command to go really meant to stay. After countering Krishna's ten challenges with eleven replies of their own, the gopis' fortitude and spiritual endurance prevailed, and Hari allowed them a dalliance that thrilled their every pore. They enjoyed beloved Hari because of their determination, wisdom, and unconditional love. The reward was showered upon them.

The gopis of Vrindavan are the bhakti gurus. Their resistance and determination are to be emulated by those who tread the fiery path of devotion. Their glories are sung among the congregations of lovers.

These stories confirm that Hari's lovers can withstand the force of their own karma, endure the effects of time and nature, and face the fires of devotion. This allows them to arrive at the beloved's door. When the delays, testing, and playing are through, the purification of the lila process makes the lover's body ready for the ultimate embrace. The bhakta-lover's body then becomes *nirguna*, devoid of any restricting worldly stuff. Then no other obstructions can delay the reunion, and there is festival after festival.

The divine pain, the affliction of not coming face to face with the beloved, is known to the rare lover. Along the way to his abode, so many things can come in the way, such as family members and other associations. They should all be withstood.

For instance, if the lover's spouse does not support the Hari romance, practice is to be done alone. Only in cases of severe opposition does the lover seek other quarters where the relationship can be expanded and explored in peace. In the case of non-support for the devotional practice, the lover of Hari should not leave the home, for the complications involved in that could exceed the problems of the home life, due to poor association and impure food. In all cases, in loss or gain, the lover never forsakes perseverance.

When there is alleviation and things work out
because of his wish, do not resist the accomplishment.
Endure false attacks from your spouse,
family members, and other people. 7

When there is a solution and the beloved removes her suffering, the lover is not too obstinate or overly righteous about those changes. The lover is not stubborn about leaving the home in her quest for the beloved. She sees all as the beloved's lila, and thus all events in her life are endured. In every situation, Hari is the refuge.

If one's worldly partner is indifferent to the beloved, let it be. The lover never forsakes compassion for all her associates. She wishes for everyone to enjoy the victory, yet if there is no divine inclination, she never resorts to being inflexible or overly righteous in any situation. In struggle with anyone, animosity becomes the bhakta's poison and always delays the ultimate festival.

When the festival is delayed—or even worse, forgotten—or when the senses focus on other things and don't remember Hari, such diversions obstruct the flow of nectar. When one's attention turns towards the beloved, the senses can be devotionally employed in the romance. She can make him garlands, prepare him sandalwood paste and offer many other treats. These offerings are then taken as *prasada*, his grace. What is pure, delightful and offered consecrates the bhakta within and without and adorns her with virtues and ornaments. The beloved keeps his eye on these.

It deepens as the lover becomes absorbed into the dharma and drama of the beloved. Then, things do not necessarily have to be renounced; they are simply given up, offered and then enjoyed again. The beloved returns the offerings. In the beloved's pleasure, divine enjoyment for all participants is one of the blessed rewards. The divine pain and its deliverance are seen as either Hari's examination or events arising because of past karmas.

When the divine body is entered and used to traverse and serve in the beloved's realms of lila pleasure, there are no more delays. That divine body is the bhakta's greatest asset and is used for the beloved's pleasure. By just understanding that the cause and supplier of all things is the beloved, everything is offered back and never employed for any self-gain. This is liberation.

In worldly matters, complications can arise from anywhere. Dilemmas can occur because of something that is desired but not received. The *mayic* possibilities are endless. Whatever the case, the true lover will not direct negative emotion towards any sentient being. She knows it is disruptive to not only the Hari relationship, but to Hari's lila creation as well.

As the lover's relationship deepens, there is a change in the way she relates to people in her world. In this divine process, sometimes people not sensitive to the transformation become jealous. They are not seeing the process. Even if they aggressively confront the lover, she withstands the attacks and keeps her attention on the beloved.

Conflicts can arise in the workplace or any other circumstances where wealth is distributed. Even if these aggressions have no cause and are clearly contrary to the higher sensitivities of dharma, the lover will not lower herself to engage at the level of her aggressors. She understands the protective aura of the beloved and endures.

This ability to withstand all situations extends to her relationships with other associates of the beloved who, because of some negligence or personal trait, turn upon their fellow lover. Still, she does not falter in her position toward Hari. When everything is seen as a play of karma that is working itself out for a higher cause, the lover is able to refrain from anger, even while withstanding the force of suffering.

Devotional fortitude is what allows the lover this ability. Hari's perfect connection to all things remains her focus. She sees him just before her as well as on both sides. In that blessed state, she employs her devotional perspectives to avoid and transform all negativities.

The illumination of the beloved's presence is the lover's protective shield.

Sense activities that are not connected to Hari
should be renounced with mind, body, and speech.
Even if one is powerless, renunciation should be done
understanding that the power to do so
8 *is not one's own, but his.*
In the powerless position, remember that Hari is everything
and that entirety is attained through refuge.
Thus I have spoken of fortitude.

When there is bhava for the beloved, there is knowledge of how much the senses should enjoy or refrain from enjoyment. When discursive senses disrupt the balance, the lover makes the necessary adjustments with a mind and heart directed towards divine engagement.

Discord arises when one's devotional sensitivities are displaced, which can lead to weakness in the bhakta's ability to handle situations skillfully. These weaknesses can arise because of a loss, but the lover knows in her devotional heart that everything is the beloved's lila. Endurance and seeing the vast scope of his lila give her, in every situation, the true view. Then all is seen as his. The lover recognizes her distinctive part and gives an outstanding performance.

Anxiety arises when the lila is forgotten, when acting is inconsistent with the higher self. Sorrow is the result of a poor performance, when the director's cues are not taken.

The implementation of small self towards shallow goals is a formula for distress. Seeing the beloved's dance in all things and accepting his amazing movement is freedom. It makes the bhakta fearless.

Some people are able to relieve their own suffering, while others can transcend it. When there is inability to do either, because one is in a powerless state, then taking the shelter of the beloved is the practice and the reward. He is *dīna dayāla*—compassionate to the humble. When the beloved's amazing nature is fathomed, the lover rests forever in his blissful embrace.

Now I will introduce
the third teaching, which is refuge in Hari. 9
In this world, or in any other,
and in every situation, Shri Hari is the refuge.
In pain and loss, in sin or in fear,
in the non-obtainment of the object of desire, 10
in anger towards other bhaktas, in the absence of devotion,
in the case of other bhaktas being aggressive with you,
in the powerless state, as well as in the position of power,
always remember that Shri Hari is the refuge. 11

When she is truly ready for him, the lover discovers the beloved's shelter everywhere. His romance and service become the true dharma, the dharma of her inner soul. For that blessed one, other activities then begin to feel unrelated. Her activities are never undertaken for any other gain. She knows unrelated karmas will create a delay. They will create separation from her beloved, which are snags in sustaining his pleasure.

With devotion, everything in the lover's life becomes connected; her life becomes simplified and transformed. Now, the lover's only effort is to submit to her beloved's aspirations. She arranges the palace of her home and heart and anticipates his early arrival. All other activities are seen as diversions.

Even if the lover experiences a state of weakness, the protector, Hari, stands beside her and makes her situation lila perfect. She sources all of her power into Hari and crosses everything else on her way to him. She reflects upon every condition in relationship to her beloved Hari, who is blissful, the remover of her obstructions and the destroyer of her sorrows.

His grace and compassion are inspiring. She finds refuge in his sidelong glance and feels worthy. In his inviting shelter, she no longer manipulates anything. She resides in a loving world and knows the perfection of his will.

By renouncing false ego, she becomes replete with humility. In that rare mood of being both firm and gentle, she surrenders to the lila and lives happily. By his grace, she attains refuge effortlessly and without any sense of self-attainment.

She now sees and feels him everywhere, at all times and in every occurrence. There is nowhere else to go. Loss, gain, fear, wealth, poverty—none of these affect her, for she is in love. She is perfectly focused and oblivious simultaneously. Her reactions to events are different than the reactions of those who have not yet fallen for him. Her romance is developed. Every occurrence is just another exchange with the beloved. Even if others are displeased with her, she does not focus on their annoyance, but upon his pleasure. The lover cannot leave the beloved even when she feels that she is not worthy of his embrace. It is the ultimate addiction.

Anxiety is never her response to pain that arises in her body or senses. Her reaction is refuge. To every circumstance, whether it is pure or impure, whether it arose before she became a lover, out of apathy, or after the true romance began, adjustments are made not with a sense of atonement, but out of love. She accomplishes everything by simply relying on him and knowing that her beloved can do no wrong. She allows herself to be enveloped in his presence and emulates those who already are.

One in refuge cannot be antagonized, nor does she have a false sense of accomplishment. She simply has no time for these things. Her every response, even if in a state of adversity, glows with refuge. She is unshakable. Even if she feels that her devotion lacks sufficient bhava, instead of experiencing guilt, she feels separation from the beloved, which makes her devotion burn even brighter.

In excessiveness or in shortcomings, whatever the situation, everything is merged into the single sweet refuge. It is at once the means and the final attainment. What more to say? Her view is refined; she finds him in every soul. Her love deepens when she remembers his other blessed ones. This refuge is self-fulfilling.

In the creation of false pride, in the
protection and nourishment of those who need sustenance,
in violations from those who are being nourished,
as well as in the transgressions of students, 12
or even in the perfection of the divine heart-mind,
always take Hari's refuge in every situation.
Maintain this sensibility firmly in the mind,
and praise it with the voice. 13

The lover of Hari relies on him always, in every way. The beloved always delivers. During difficult times or false identifications, when people trespass, in accomplishment or failure, in fame or dishonor, the lover beholds all passings of life as gifts from God.

Even in the state of perfection, humility is never forsaken. With the beloved's glance upon her, she feels his proximity in all things and then fully understands that he will not forsake her. She revels in the romance and speaks of it in the circle of his other lovers.

Relationships can turn dark, even between lovers, but feelings of regret and woe are overcome with a higher remembrance. When there is true reliance, the beloved responds by allowing his presence to be felt throughout the lover's world. That cognition, his mere remembrance, sunders useless identifications. In that blessed state, even when the bhakta is treated improperly by family members, friends, or by those she supports, or during times of injustice, she never resorts to anger. She sees that to do so would only drag her away from the beloved's sacred realm.

The lover's mind, her heart, and her cognition, both inward and outward, are filled with devotion. Her world is sacred. Her bhava for Hari, the exalted heart-mind state, protects her from the forces of non-related thought and activities that bring distance and forgetfulness. She removes all spiritual disloyalty, and as she soars to her beloved's realm, she is filled with the illumination of his presence. Even in perfection, divine passion rules and keeps her refuge firm and enduring.

The blessed experience of the beloved is occasionally revealed. Sometimes it is shown openly and at other times in guarded fashion with those who share in the lover's banquet.

When the beloved is spoken of, he appears. His name and form are inseparable. This is another secret to his presence.

When the lover is not prepared to meet with her beloved, she reaches out for him and takes his protective shelter by calling out his name. She recites mantra. She calls out, "Shri Krishna is my refuge, Shri Krishna is my refuge." Her recitations sweeten and prepare her devotional heart.

The beloved's name first arises on the tongue and then goes to the throat. Then it fills the mind before overflowing into the heart. Finally it resounds in every pore, replete with the sublime yearning, "You are mine." It is a continuous and perfect habit. Krishna enjoys it.

As the lover's love deepens, she no longer desires to go anywhere else. She feels that not only is her spiritual heart wed to him, but even the welfare of her material existence is in his hands. Now, no other can stand between them.

It is also forbidden to worship another, or
to pray to another for any of your work to be done. 14

Lovers of Hari only resort to the beloved. To leave him is to forget one's true self. It is an act of suspicion and constitutes a contradiction of the devotional heart. It is a move away from his sacred space, a turning away from all forms of perfection. It is illicit. The lover with true abandonment in him could never do such a thing! To leave the beloved and look elsewhere is the result of deception, or *maya*. It arises when the senses no longer see the true object, when vision is blurred. Faulty cognition poisons devotion.

Without bhakti, people wander elsewhere to find satisfaction and hook up with insignificant beloveds who cannot provide. When the authentic beloved is forgotten, the result is bondage.

When everything appears from him, how can there be any question about Hari's integrity? The lover does not water the leaves; she goes directly to the root. Otherwise, desires then turn to hankerings, and in the cracks of confidence, the devotional essence is lost.

Someone might object, "But it is not right to go to the beloved for all things. To approach him for everything would be troublesome. The lover should go to the lesser forces, to the other devas, for simple needs."

The lover explains, "I am only engaged to Hari and can have no other romance. My beloved protects me in all circumstances. I cannot dilute nor divide devotion. The nature of nectar is singular, and bhakti attains its zenith when it is one-pointed."

When the lover adores the beloved, that adoration merges with his love and is felt everywhere. It is a state of total love where Hari's presence is felt in all things and at all times and places. The lover is bathed in perfect unity. For her, there is no cause great enough to ever justify abandoning that connection for another.

The bhaktas of Braja—the gopis, the gurus of devotion who had attained love, attachment, and addiction—prayed to Hari. But their requests to Krishna were special. Even if they requested their beloved to remove a forest fire, or to stop Indra from showering his rains, their root supplication was to attain the continual shelter of his feet. They could withstand the forest blaze, but they were consumed by the fire of separation from his lotus feet.

Prayers for his love, a request for his presence, for his lotus feet, are not the same as prayers for worldly prosperity. The lover cannot engage in the world without him. Her pleas are for the rendezvous.

The lover's requests have special meanings. Bhaktas do not pray for self-protection. Their song arises out of longing for their beloved. There is never any self-gain or worldly design in their supplication.

The village of Gokul is the bhaktas' town and their reward. Hari arrives there with the sole purpose of lila. He becomes the award-giver and responds to the bhava of his bhaktas. The beloved overflows with elixir and, according to the vessel, fills his loved ones with his essential being.

The beloved's play appears to be just like the world, but unlike common, mundane manifestation, everything about Hari is replete with divine meaning and wonder.

When the beloved decides to create a particular play, to perform a certain lila, everything necessary arises. The beloved's acts and engagements are for the highest lila purpose; they are filled with incredible dharma. His bhaktas understand this and act accordingly. The beloved plays in such a way that his lovers become enveloped in him. Their prayers and aspirations are all for his benefit and are replete with lila meaning.

Even after the lover renounces everything except her beloved's sanctuary, he still acts according to his own will.

Never lose faith.
If you do, it will impede your every situation.

Understand lack of faith from the story of Hanuman,
who broke free from the powerful Brahmastra weapon
because his captors lost faith in it.
Understand faith from the tale of the chataka bird, who
forsakes all waters except the rain drops from certain clouds.
Perform seva, his pleasing worship,
with whatever is obtained
15 *and without false sense of ownership.*

When weak spiritual conviction strikes the devotional heart, it breeds uncertainty, clouds clarity, and brings about a host of obstructions that gather before the bhakta on her way to the beloved. Two examples are given: one of faith, the other of doubt. In every case, false identification regarding attainment should be renounced.

When the beloved is disregarded because of a break in trust, it is due to a lack of understanding the nature of the beloved. It ruins the subtle dharma of refuge, and then certainty in all matters is lost. With loving power gone, the discursive mind takes control.

An example of lack of faith is found in the story of Hanuman, the great monkey god, son of the wind and perfect Ram bhakta. Lord Hanuman went to Sri Lanka in search of Ram's wife, Shri Sita. There, the demon King Ravana, knowing of Hanuman's arrival, had his powerful son Indrajit ensnare Hanuman with a mystic invincible weapon, the Brahmastra. Hanuman was immediately contained by its spell.

Part of the mystic nature of the Brahmastra weapon is that its binding cords cannot be seen. The others, seeing Lord Hanuman apparently captured, but without any sign of shackles, decided to further secure him with some ordinary ropes, thus disregarding the rarefied powers of the Brahmastra weapon. They were unaware of the fact that as soon as a doubt is placed over the Brahmastra, it immediately loses its effect. With the power of the Brahmastra diminished, Lord Hanuman freed himself and wreaked havoc over Sri Lanka before returning to Lord Ram, who was ultimately able to rescue his beloved Sita.

The teaching is direct. If a practitioner loses faith in refuge, then the power as well as the dharma of his shelter is lost. With the cords of love sundered, the untrusting heart wanders. When the heart becomes divided in dedication, the essence is lost. In the divide, an opening is formed and the nectar seeps out, sometimes unnoticed.

The mystical chataka bird is a guru of conviction. This amazing bird refuses all other waters except for rainwater that falls only during a fifteen-day autumnal lunar cycle. Besides those rains, the chataka bird will taste no other water, regardless of its source. It has set its heart on the one.

Because of the bird's faith in those clouds, regardless of circumstance, when the time is right the clouds shower rain for that blessed bird. It is the chataka bird's confidence and trust in those waters that brings about the downpour. Similarly, the lover has all of her sacred desires quenched by the beloved. Her faith allows her to see that Hari makes all that is necessary arise. Her conviction produces unshakable refuge and brings an end to all other hankerings. She knows that what is needed is obtained without effort. Once attained, no false sense of ownership is placed upon anything.

With the understanding of Hari's desire, the false ego is dissolved and "myness" no longer prevails. All circumstances, relations, attainments, and everything that comes into the lover's life are used for him.

In all undertakings, whether they be high or low,
religious or worldly, maintain the bhava that
"Shri Hari is my refuge."
16 *What more is there to say?*
Thus I have spoken of refuge in Hari,
which is at all times beneficial to all.
In my opinion, bhakti and other practices
are difficult to perform in this age of struggle,
17 *and therefore, one should take to the path of refuge.*

The lover goes about her way, doing what she has to do throughout her world. She is always free of expectations. Whatever is required of her, even in worldly spheres, is seen as the command of her beloved, even if it does not appear to be directly connected to him. Everything is justified. She never loses sight of him. The Hari romance is never forgotten. She never confuses dharmas or priorities; her life revolves around the beloved.

In the *Bhagavad Gita*, after Arjuna had imbibed Shri Krishna's wisdom, he realized that he had to fight the battle. He could only do so with Hari's remembrance. Even though he was engaged in a dreadful conflict, Arjuna never forgot his essential refuge and connection.

The teachings put forth here are that the bhakta should undergo everything, whether worldly, religious, or whatever it may be, without hypocrisy or any sense of self-attainment, while resting in Hari's shelter. Those lovers who maintain devotional balance in all scenarios set examples for others and, like Arjuna, move to victory.

The dharma of refuge is not dependent upon the performance of any particular karma. The dharma of refuge is a state of being. It is the root of all dharmas and can be found everywhere, in all undertakings. To the lover, this is apparent. It is the heart of the yogas; it is their inner secret.

Non-lovers cannot see, although it is unmistakably clear. The bhakta-poet Nandadas says it all:

A lamp is not lit by discussion,
but by being ignited.

It is a matter of taking refuge to heart. The devotional policy is about experience, never worldly gain. All is done in order to be invited to the beloved's abode. Then the beloved's endorsement is found everywhere.

All is attained when there is freedom from vested interest. Then the lover feels her beloved in all things. Her consciousness is alert when she remembers that he could appear at any moment. She is forever ready. This sweet mixture of union and separation keeps her above the common law.

Even if she is diverted, the path is easily found again through refuge. In the heights of devotion, the lover leaves all dharmas and finds their source, called *dharmi*. That source is her beloved, the remover of all impediments.

Refuge is always rewarding. It can be felt by anyone who is able to put down their guard long enough to feel the beloved's effect. Refuge is the foundation upon which the advanced bhakti practices have been established. Without refuge, bhakti yoga is impossible to practice. That is why Shri Mahaprabhuji stresses refuge.

Refuge can begin at any place, from any stage or condition in life. Refuge is a practice that is open to all and is capable of granting anything, anywhere. As its effects are effortless and spontaneous, once they are realized, all other campaigns are discarded. In the past there could be achievement through practices like tantra, pujas, meditations, and other sadhanas. One great virtue of this current age, the Kali Yuga, is that simply through the name and refuge of Hari, there is perfect attainment. Since this era is impure and laced with strife, practices often become filled with hypocrisy and other confusions that keep the beloved away.

In the current impure age of Kali, circumstances are not conducive to pure devotion. The sacred forms have become hidden. That is why the emphasis is upon refuge, as it is the foundation of devotion.

With the influence of grace, there is a gentle push from the beloved that allows the lover to swing to the heights of his abode. This refuge is not blind. It must embrace the attitude that the beloved lives within all things, and that divine presence must be sought after and experienced everywhere. Only then can the mystery and union of shelter be reached. Merely saying, "I am yours" without feeling it, and without sensing the beloved personally, will not bring about true refuge of the spiritual heart. When that mood is penetrated, the lover's single step is followed by ten of his. Then the lover looks for him everywhere and begins to see.

These are some of the inner moods of refuge that lovers cherish everywhere and at all times. It is not only a secret doctrine, but the marriage contract between beloved Hari and his sensitive, bhakti yogi lover.

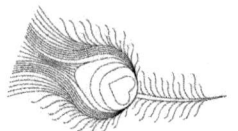

About the Translator

Shyamdas (1953-2013), the respected and accomplished Vaishnava bhakti practitioner, translator, teacher, and kirtan singer, first traveled to India in 1972, mysticly summoned by the saint "Maharaji" Neem Karoli Baba. Shyamdas's devotional life continued to blossom with the guidance of his pushtimarg guru, Goswami Shri Prathameshji, 17th generation descendant of Shri Vallabhacharya and head of Pratham Peeth, the first house of the lineage. Shyamdas lived and studied in India for decades, imbibing the nectars of devotion and distilling ancient teachings for modern audiences. His insightful translations bring the spiritual teachings and poetry of the pushti bhakti masters to life for English readers worldwide.

www.ShyamdasFoundation.com

www.ingramcontent.com/pod-product-compliance
Lightning Source LLC
Chambersburg PA
CBHW030635150426
42811CB00077B/2110/J
* 9 7 8 0 9 7 4 6 7 6 8 1 4 *